soultrader

DO WHO

YOU ARE

soultrader

find purpose and you'll find success

Carmel McConnell

www.yourmomentum.com
the stuff that drives you

What is momentum?

Momentum is a completely new publishing philosophy, in print and online, dedicated to giving you more of the information, inspiration and drive to enhance who you are, what you do, and how you do it.

Fusing the changing forces of work, life and technology, momentum will give you the right stuff for a brighter future and set you on the way to being all you can be.

Who needs momentum?

Momentum is for people who want to make things happen in their careers and their lives, who want to work at something they enjoy and that's worthy of their talents and their time.

Momentum people have values and principles, and question who they are, what they do, and who for. Wherever they work, they want to feel proud of what they do. And they are hungry for information, stimulation, ideas and answers ...

Momentum online

Visit *www.yourmomentum.com* to be part of the talent community. Here you'll find a full listing of current and future books, an archive of articles by momentum authors, sample chapters and self-assessment tools. While you're there, post your work/life questions to our momentum coaches and sign up to receive free newsletters with even more stuff to drive you.

more momentum

If you need more drive for your life, try one of these other momentum titles:

mental space
how to find clarity in a complex life
Carmel McConnell

reinvent yourself
tactics for work, life and happiness – yours
J. Jonathan Gabay

be your own career consultant
unlock your career potential and help yourself to your future
Gary Pyke and Stuart Neath

managing brand me
how to build your personal brand
Thomas Gad and
Anette Rosencreutz

coach yourself
make real change in your life
Anthony M. Grant and Jane Greene

change activist
make big things happen fast
Carmel McConnell

lead yourself
be where others will follow
Mick Cope

happy mondays
putting the pleasure back into work
Richard Reeves

innervation
redesign yourself for a smarter future
Guy Browning

the big difference
life works when you choose it
Nicola Phillips

hey you!
pitch to win in an ideas economy
Will Murray

snap, crackle or stop
change your career and create your own destiny
Barbara Quinn

float you
how to capitalize on your talent
Carmel McConnell and Mick Cope

from here to e
equip yourself for a career in the wired economy
Lisa Khoo

grow your personal capital
what you know, who you know and how you use it
Hilarie Owen

PEARSON EDUCATION LIMITED

Head Office
Edinburgh Gate
Harlow CM20 2JE
Tel: +44 (0)1279 623623
Fax: +44 (0)1279 431059

London Office:
128 Long Acre
London WC2E 9AN
Tel: +44 (0)20 7447 2000
Fax: +44 (0)20 7240 5771
Website: www.yourmomentum.com

First published in Great Britain in 2002

The right of Carmel McConnell to be identified as Author of this Work has been asserted by her in accordance with the Copyright, Designs and Patents Act 1988.

ISBN 1843 04018 2

British Library Cataloguing in Publication Data
A CIP catalogue record for this book can be obtained from the British Library.

10 9 8 7 6 5 4 3 2 1

Typeset by Northern Phototypesetting Co. Ltd, Bolton
Printed and bound in Great Britain by Henry Ling Ltd, Dorchester

Production design by
Claire Brodmann Book Designs,
Lichfield, Staffs

The Publishers' policy is to use paper manufactured from sustainable forests.

thank you …

Thank you to my mum and dad for actively continuing to love and help me, thank you to Catherine for encouraging with time and love even when other things were more urgent, to my wonderful sister Carolyn for being so optimistic, to my editor and dare I say friend, Rachael Stock, for saying unjustifiably kind things about early drafts and always having brilliant advice, thank you to Mick Cope for endless support and mind-altering ideas, to Dave and Heather for their generous insight and, once again, loan of their home in Fowey (surely the last time?), to Judy Purkiss for her practical, inspiring goodness, to Jimmy and Nora, to Josie and Tom, to Mrs McCurley and Sister Francis at Sacred Heart Convent School who said God wants us to be happy, thank you to Gillian Gargett, because her friendship is so important to me, to Wendy Briner for expecting more of my mind than I ever did, to my family in Fermanagh who know I will get home as soon as this is finished (promise), to the team working on the Magic Sandwich project, especially Karen Drury, Elana and Sofia, to Paul Steggall, Helen Albany and the team at carbon for their help and farsighted business philosophy, to the momentum team at Long Acre, particularly ideas whizzes Elie Ball, Russell Fairbanks and Rachel Russell. Thank you to everyone who opened their hearts and souls for book interviews, completing the www.yourmomentum.com websurvey, thank you to others who have helped me realize soultrading can bring success in any profession, for any kind of person. Finally, thank you to all those who have contributed through discussions and random e-mails – I really appreciate all you have done to help.

the assertion

Being a soultrader is the best personal strategy for sustainable career success.

Also known as 'do who you are'.

A guess at the reader wish list:

- ◆ You want to create cash for day-to-day comfort.
- ◆ Plus inner peace and self-esteem.
- ◆ You want to believe your career is somehow worthwhile to humanity.
- ◆ You want to figure out who you are before it doesn't matter anymore.
- ◆ You hope the first two points can be tackled somewhere in the paper-thin margins between work, lurve, shopping and sleep.

why read soultrader?

Do you feel you have to go to work or you want to go to work?

Quick check. Please tick a or b.

My work feels like:

a) Draining duty

b) Creative challenge

Between 2.30pm and 4.30pm I am usually:

a) Restless, bit bored

b) Alive, sometimes inspired

Would your soul like to feel nourished by what you do for a living?
Right answer. Because there is a professional cost attached to being
uninspired by what you do. It costs when you're lost. Creatively, financially,
emotionally, fulfilmentally.

I made that last word up.

I promise to help you find your own unique recipe for career fulfilment,
regardless of your job, education, age or nationality — whatever. The
detail of where you are now is not the most important thing. What is
important is that you make the transition from where you are now to
somewhere happier, more fulfilled and more successful. You are the
priority.

My only request is that when you and I are together on this page (like we
are now) you catch the answers prompted by these words and do
something with them …

contents

how soultrader works

This book aims to help you figure life from the inside out, rather than outside in, for a change.

Soultrader is presented in six chapters:

Chapter 1 Find purpose, find success

'Being a soultrader is the best personal strategy for sustainable career success.'

'Why?'

'Because if you find purpose, you find success.'

The first chapter defines what it means to be an individual soultrader, exploring the practical side of purpose, meaning, soul and spirit. It contains lots of exercises to help you find out if your calling might be calling and getting the engaged tone. You'll find out what life purpose looks like. It features the fire and focus exercise, which could help if you have ever asked yourself, 'What do I want to be when I grow up'? (I don't care if you were 17 or 70 when you last asked this.) Also in Chapter 1 we'll spend time detecting your authentic self beneath all the 'at work, on display' layers. It sounds exhaustive but believe me, Chapter 1 is as good as a cool swim on a muggy day.

As a financial services manager, I found Chapter 1 hugely reviving.

Anonymous fictitious future reader

Chapter 2 Working a way to your soul

'Being a soultrader is the best personal strategy for sustainable career success.'

'Why?'

'Because work contains all sorts of challenges, like growth – the fact that most of us need to earn in some way forces us to grow.'

Work can be the best way to experience who you are.

Chapter 3 Personal strategies

'Being a soultrader is the best personal strategy for sustainable career success.'

'Why?'

'Because your soul knows how to create a personal career strategy. If you learn, to listen.'

The third chapter looks at personal career strategies – what works in the search for a career with profit and principles? This is the chapter that translates what you learn in Chapter 1 into your world, starting with your workplace. You may have heard that eyes are the windows of the soul. In this chapter, you will learn to use your soul as an operating system just like Windows.

Chapter 4 Make better career decisions

'Being a soultrader is the best personal strategy for sustainable career success.'

'Why?'

'Because you make better career decisions.'

Having worked out the benefits of soultrading, working with purpose, this chapter goes a stage further by giving you some career perspective. Looking at very grown-up questions like 'Should I stay or should I go?', 'How can freelancers sleep at night with a mortgage to pay?' and 'How can I create a trust-based career network?'. The chapter also considers questions such as 'Why do we go to work?', and 'Is mine an accidental career?' It also contains the Four Decisions model, a balanced set of criteria to consider your career options. Are your ambitions best served as a free agent, in or out of your current firm? How can you tell if your current job is your destiny?

Chapter 5 Work just changed. Forever

'Being a soultrader is the best personal strategy for sustainable career success.'

'Why?'

'Because the world of work just changed.'

This chapter looks at the changes to the world of work that will impact on you as you make better career decisions, energized with purpose. How we seek cool, low-hierarchy jobs, which are also structured and secure. How we seek spiritual fulfilment but also the latest electronic gadget. Technology has brought new jobs and opened new global markets, but we are in a recession. What is the impact of these seemingly irreconcilable issues on you, the decent individual? This chapter looks at how to stay fuelled in a world that is faster and more transparent. How useful are your soultrader skills in a global market? Does trust have any commercial value? Chapter 5

how soultrader works

soultrader

momentum

also looks at soultrader firms and ideas for those who want to make profits, without losing out on principles. You may want to lie down after so much excitement.

My job has been really busy so I haven't considered the big picture for a while. I had no idea.

Another fictitious future reader

Chapter 6 12-day life purpose plan

This final chapter collates the exercises and lessons into a concise programme that you can use to tailor your own soulgrowing programme. Use the programme in a team or with a friend, or take this opportunity to get to know the postman better. The consistent message is that when you are clear on who you are, you make better work/life decisions, locate more elegant career solutions, and live as your true self. How about that as a definition of success?

Soultrader style

Style wise, this could turn into intensive career/life purpose coaching if you want it to. If so, be prepared to get the biro and honesty muscle out.

Expect regular questions about your career thinking and life direction, and frank advice to help you assess your current situation with a fresh perspective. Like anything, your reward from soultrader is going to be in proportion to the time and space you invest to investigate.

It really is up to you, but I can help and am here all hours. So,

if you don't know what you want from your career, it's OK. Start here.

chapter one
find purpose, find success

'Being a soultrader is the best personal strategy for sustainable career success.'

'Why?'

'Because if you find purpose, you find success.'

Introduction

This is a practical guide on how to become happier and more fulfilled in your work and in your life. A career guide to the true you inside.

Soultrader concepts are simple:

◆ Like it or not, you are gorgeous, gifted and unique.

◆ You have a life purpose.

◆ Your life purpose is to be happy, fulfilled and successful, according to your own definition.

◆ Awakening to purpose significantly increases your chances of success – creating meaningful, inspiring, nutritious work.

- So you'll need a compass. This is your soul; always there to guide you through each decision, each career trade.

- **The soultrader is you.**

My goal is to help you get excited about your work and your life for one good reason.

Being fulfilled, animated, and true to yourself is the best strategy for career success.

Did I say that already? Well it is important.

Maybe you disagree …?

- 'I'm an investment banker and very successful. I have never worried about being true to myself. The money is true enough.'

- 'I never bother with all this navel-gazing rubbish. I'm ruling a building company with an iron fist and we're doing very nicely thank you.'

- 'Sounds lovely. But I haven't got the time or energy right now to go off and find my "true purpose" whatever that is. And what's the point anyway?'

- 'You hippies have no idea of the real world.'

These are perfectly valid sentiments. And very realistic, for some people. You, perhaps?

The banker need not have been unhappy in order to be successful, but some wrongly believe suffering is a compulsory ingredient of financial success. The builder made good is possibly garnering profit at the expense of friendship and trust – which isn't profit long term. A lonely pint for company at 60 isn't a successful life outcome.

Soultrader will show that ignoring your true purpose is the most expensive, career-limiting option.

soultrader

momentum

Leaving purpose out from your working day is a recipe for fast decline of creativity, care, stamina and hunger for learning – ultimately the ingredients of your personal competitive advantage.

Which is fine if you don't care about those things. Fine if you no longer want success with integrity, or the chance to show life what you really can do with those talents. Do those things matter to you? There is evidence that a broader definition of career success is emerging – from the rise of free agency to the stirrings of corporate social responsibility. The concept of personal responsibility for career success is mainstream.

Are you ever aware that something is going on inside you, a movement of hopes and dreams? A feeling that is more than emotion? It feels ultra-personal, yours alone. It isn't easy to describe, hard to get at. OK. This something is maybe your soul. I really don't know how this works for you. If I were in Ireland I could say it is the melody of your unique song, which you alone can hear. See what I mean about finding it hard to describe?

People sometimes refer to a calling. Your big 'I want', your life's destiny, the thing you were born to do. A career energized with worthwhile purpose. That would be nice.

You wonder when this deeper force is going to make some sensible contribution to your daily life, like telling you what you are going to be when you grow up. It is trying to. And the argument of this book is this: if you bring who you are – all of who you are – to what you are trying to do, you will uncover your purpose and clarify your reason for being here. This will be a much easier context for success at whatever career choice you make.

Draw on this internal capital in direct proportion to how much success you want in life. Your self-totality out front as career reality equals salary and holistic sanity. Your success depends on how well you access your personal, spiritual capital. Not that I like putting those words alongside each other necessarily!

I think if you don't look after it then no amount of mone

happy.

Rachel Russell, assista

Soultrading is essential. That is, it is of your essence.

A life expressing the true you in everything you do. The truer you are
the more fuelled you are. More fuel equals more performance power.
More performance power equals more double portions twice kind of
life. Do you want double portions twice achievement? Double portions
twice fulfilment? Double portions twice challenge? Double portions
twice enlightenment? Then your career route needs to begin with your
innermost.

Soultrading is also about transactions. Each career phase involves a
trade. Trade brain, get salary. Trade good attitude, get happy peers.
Trade track record, get promotion and a bigger challenge. Soultrading
is a verb. To soultrade is to be actively engaged in shaping your
destiny, to design your life with more purpose and clarity. More you
inside. Your soul is the inner limit of the universe and if you can listen
to directions from there, you have no outer limits.

Soultrading is the future. I may be understating this.

Purpose is unique for each one of us, and subject to our
emotional and financial position in our lives. If we are
agoraphobic, going outside on our own may be a great purpose.
If we have been stuck in a job for 20 years finding the self
esteem and courage to change may be our purpose. Each of us
has something that our spirit is calling us to do that will take us
beyond our perceived limitations.

Nick Williams, *The work we were born to do*

Soultrading will increase your capacity to succeed, to move upward
and onwards. Why? Because soultraders know who they are and
what they are trying to achieve in life. That translates into myriad
career advantages. Soultraders do the following:

- **Make better career choices – for example, knowing what
  constitutes a 'good fit'.** If you knew your life's purpose was to
  reduce suffering, would you take a job as a golf caddie? Or would
  you take a job as a corporate crisis counsellor? Or less
  dramatically, if family time was important, would you take a
  consulting role in Singapore? Only if you wanted divorce. Your
  best decision would be to take the job most likely to lead to
  fulfilment and happiness. You can't beat happiness, really.

- **Negotiate the grey areas.** Most jobs have fairly clearly defined
  objectives and responsibilities. These were a necessity for the tight
  management style of hierarchical command and control
  structures. Input, output, measures and all that. Nowadays,
  although structure and targets are still important, your ability to
  contribute all your fast-thinking talent is paramount, and should
  the traditional job arrangements fail to support your personal
  style and performance, it is up to you to negotiate. This is more
  acceptable and widespread than you think. And it is much, much
  easier to negotiate with confidence when you are clear about who
  you are and what is important to you. In fact, soultraders expect
  to negotiate and fine tune to create the optimum career situation.

One example of successful negotiation:

Working for someone who cares and is interested in what I do, who measures my performance and rewards me (not just monetary but tells me when I'm doing well). Working for someone who gives me the freedom to do what I think is best for the role, best for the team and for the company. Also working flexibly (i.e. up to three days a week at home) really makes me happy! I get so much more done when I'm at home and don't have the two-hour commute each way.

Heather Shand, Manager, DB HR Delivery Team BP (global energy company)

◆ **Build trust among colleagues, customers and friends.** Trust is faster and stronger than any set of contracts or service level agreements. This translates to speed to market, better supplier relations and more motivated employees. You name it. The soultrader, in the act of choosing his or her life's work, is more likely to want to make it work. A key part of that will be to strengthen relationships because they feel true and right. The soultrader therefore has natural advantage. How would you rate, trustwise, with colleagues right now?

◆ **Take risks to get things done.** Athletes talk about being in the zone – where there is total alignment of mental and physical energies. In that moment, risk is no longer risk, it is an exciting challenge. Soultraders are brave because they have the sense that this is the work they were born to do. How do you imagine that feels?

◆ **Give their chosen work 100%.** Similarly, when you connect your innermost hopes with your outer career activities, a kind of freedom emerges. Freedom to put everything you have into making it happen. The contribution made by someone just to earn some cash doesn't even come close. And which do you think makes a bigger difference to the overall goal?

◆ **Lead and motivate with authenticity, not by company mantra.**
This is where the soultrader advantage is perhaps most
noticeable. The fact that your work has meaning for you and
gives you a sense of accomplishment and fulfilment will, in itself,
create role-model behaviour. You can't fake happy, you can fake
cheerful. You can't fake conviction, you can fake enthusiasm.
Subtle differences, yes, but when you have a team who look you
in the eyes and want to learn, they will want to know that their
leader is a soultrader. Trust me.

PRACTICAL SOULSEARCHING

What do you spend your time wishing for?

**"With recent budget cuts, he's the best
motivation speaker we could get."**

So how can you get that soultrader career advantage? All it is
going to take is a little investment in yourself, a little excavation.
You have all the answers right now. My job is to help you uncover
them.

Let's start with a definition.

Defining your soul

Soul = spirit, essence, life, vitality, animation, essential quality, core

Trader = business person, retailer, merchant, wholesaler

To soultrade: *verb*

To achieve personal fulfilment in work and in life. The deployment of personal strategies to achieve lasting career success.

Soultrader: *noun*

Person who understands and employs the vital animating force within to achieve career fulfilment. Also, person energized with purpose, on the road to personal fulfilment, wealth and happiness.

A root-and-branch analysis of your life

Any analogy can seem cheesy, but given that we are seeking to understand the somewhat intangible concepts of soul and purpose, I want to save you excess headscratching and bewilderment. Here goes.

We have agreed that your soul is the vital, animating force within. It is deeper than values, broader than current attitudes.

Like a tree has to have roots to survive, we need soul to provide our underpinning, our foundation. Like a tree branches out and bears fruit, our lives articulate the contents of our head, heart and hand through our actions. Like a tree has to grow to survive, the soul has to have space in your life to expand. Bearing fruit requires an intake of nutrition through the roots, transported through every branch, every twig, every leaf. Sustainable career success results from attention to each area of our lives, our health, our relationships, our development. Not just our e-mails.

This tree is your life, your soul its roots, basis, reason, source; your career directions are its branches, your values its sap, your success its fruit; all interdependent and fundamentally connected. The tree has to change according to season and is dramatically impacted by changes to environment. The healthy tree is, I hope, a ripe analogy for genuine career success. You are more likely to succeed by keeping your soul healthy, keeping your vital animating force as a precious resource to nourish everything you plan to do.

Branching out

At any time in your career you've only got one of two decisions to make. Either stay, or go.

Let me explain.

The soultrader tree has many branches, each signifying a possible career direction, but in terms of major structure (and therefore overall career decisions) there are just two stems from the trunk. One is stay where you are, the other leave and do something else. Assuming that as a soultrader you will be actively seeking happiness, fulfilment and success, at any one time in your working life you can decide to do one of those two things.

Stay divides into two branches. Go divides into two branches, as you can see on the tree.

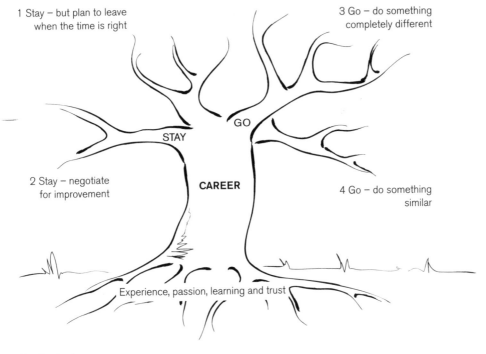

1 Stay – but plan to leave
when the time is right

3 Go – do something
completely different

GO

STAY

2 Stay – negotiate
for improvement

CAREER

4 Go – do something
similar

Experience, passion, learning and trust

Soultrader tree

So you have four options.

1   Stay (but realize this is pretransition)

Be open to the idea that your career is in transition and be ready
to take action when the time is right. For example, the person who
has family priorities outside work, who chooses to keep things
stable, planning to move in time.

2   Stay and negotiate

Within the current situation, to make improvements and stay. For
example, if you are a freelance computer programmer, you could
ask your client to allow you to work from home one day per
week.

3   Leave for a new but similar job

Move to a new job in the same field, to be closer to what feels like
life purpose: a branch that subdivides into the many kinds of new

roles open to you. For example, if you are a public relations manager, you could become a corporate communications manager in a firm that feels more right for you.

4 **Leave for something completely different**

Create something completely different for yourself: a branch that subdivides into all the many possibilities. For example, the unqualified uberlad who became a stand-up comedian and then TV presenter then social pundit. Quite a common one that.

A few other ideas on branches.

If you prune, you'll have more fruit.

Remember this one. It might also add zest to the team meeting.

Where the tree is allowed to extend and extend, the branches themselves take all the goodness from the sap, leaving none for the growing fruit. A lesson to those of us who like to overcommit and overextend. Perhaps we should lop off some of the excess activities that leave us depleted when it comes to our main purpose. That being fruit, i.e. happiness, fulfilment, success.

Roots

Quick natural history moment – trees take their nutrition from the soil via the roots. Sap (a juice-like liquid) is sucked upward between layers of bark. Sap delivers vital minerals and water to the growing branches, twigs and leaves. And, as you may have heard, it rises in spring.

Roots are the tree's anchor, the source of stability.

Grow strong roots in yourself as a person. Not your job description.

Generally speaking, if you cut the root deeply, the tree will die. Cut the branch, and it tends to survive. In the same way, without any sense of soul or life purpose, your career will wither.

Many career branches can grow when they are supported by a healthy tree with strong roots.

It is interesting to note that the tree holding its leaves late into the season is at most risk of being uprooted in a storm – the roots are weak because nutrition is still going to the leaves. This was evident in the great UK storm of 1987 when (I am reliably informed) felled trees were more likely to be those still in leaf. This is perhaps a reminder to let go of old ways of doing things, outdated attitudes or skills when the time is right. Or risk weakening your whole career. Tree. Thing.

Back at the analogy, the soultrader tree has four major roots, including one leader root. The roots are how you'll be nourished to grow those branches, to create fruits of success. I can't find a true sounding analogy for the leader root. If you do, please get in touch via www.yourmomentum.com. Sign it cleverclogs. Thank you.

Soul most tangibly manifests as a sense of life purpose. The four roots of that purpose are:

1 Experience (subdivided into the roots of knowledge, skills and attitude).

2 Learning (subdivided into the roots of risk taking and wonder).

3 Passion (subdivided into the roots of action, choice and change).

4 Trust (subdivided into the roots of confidence, expectation and patience).

More on this later.

Soil

The tree will grow well in good soil. Over planting, i.e. too many trees placed in the same area of soil and with limited light, will result in the depletion of the soil's natural richness, which will result in a stunting of tree growth or loss of fruit. Unless you feed the soil. Likewise, your career will flourish with access to resources to support growth, such as an environment that supports your learning, a management structure that has space for you to stretch out and try new things.

Generally speaking, the tree extracts minerals and water from the soil, and replaces the same or more through the fertilizing activities of the birds and squirrels, who become part of the living tree community. Plus, of course, the natural regeneration caused by falling leaves – pointing to the need for a good natural environment for your soultrader tree, aka your career, to grow. It also suggests that it is a good idea to replenish your environment in order to grow.

Soil erosion happens when there are no trees and the force of elements, rain and wind conspire to erode the topsoil, exposing the underlying sand, which, without the attachment of roots, blows away. Hence deforestation can quickly transform a green landscape, rich with topsoil, to barren mountainous terrain. Last year I went to a rainforest project in Ecuador and drove through dismal brown hills that had, 20 years ago, been primary rainforest. It was depressing.

In the same way, though obviously not so critical to the planet, an exodus of you and I would depopulate previously thriving industrial landscapes, leaving them high and dry. Which is what nearly happened to consulting firms and big corporates at the height of the dot.com boom. (Maybe some of the dot.coms tried to become giant redwoods atop the roots of a geranium, causing them to fall as cooler economic winds blew through the valley.)

Before we leave this analogy and we get back to your career, I have to tell you about one more tree. It lives far away, it is called the walking palm, and it is a native of the Amazonian rainforests in South America. The walking palm can move roots to transport the whole tree to another location, with more light, space and soil nutrients. The roots quite literally walk to a better spot. I'm not talking about a day trip to Texas, mind you, but up to a metre during its lifetime. A natural free agent perhaps?

Fruit

Finally. The healthy tree produces fruit in direct proportion to the environment, the soil, and the amount of proportionate branching out. Fruit contains the seeds of new trees, the minerals and vitamins to feed the community abound and tastes good. The analogy here is to say that fruit is necessary to provide the refreshment for more growth, necessary to seed future ventures.

What do you consider to be the fruits of your labour right now? The car? The feelgood factor sorting out a customer query? The feel of wind in your hair as you chase escaping sheep? A healthy career bears fruit.

So there is the soultrader analogy. You can grow and branch out, depending on the health of your roots.

Your career will grow and thrive, provided your roots are allowed to help. Your soul, your vital animating force within, can't be a force unless you recognize the connection.

Did it work for you? OK. Hoping that was a yes, I'll move on.

How do soultraders get nourishment from their environment, their soil? Are they strong above ground level, i.e. their career face, because of the depth of foundation below ground, i.e. soul level purpose?

Each root draws nutrition into your working life. The root of experience allows us to grow into a new job in less time than if we had no previous experience. The root of passion gives urgency to our actions. The root of learning enables us to keep searching for answers and remain open to new things. The final root, the root of trust, places our expectation, calmly, on success. There are many subroots, of course. These roots keep digging deeper for even more nutrition, seeking out work that provides more challenge, stimuli and rewards.

Roots and soul are similar in that their value doesn't seem too great until they are in trouble.

The tree changes according to the season, it grows and eventually loses each new leaf, each fruit. The branches extend and add additional foliage. Each bifurcation adds beauty. Roots remain constant, allowing the tree to continue through the demands of each seasonal change. In the same way, your career is going to involve times of growth, of stability, of loss. The key is to keep your roots healthy, able to sustain your sense of purpose in whatever season.

Storms make trees take deeper root.

George Herbert

As we go through the book, the soultrader tree will help illustrate the aspects of our working life, such as career direction (the four main choices when we want to literally branch out) and the four primary roots of our success. The goal with your life, as with the tree, is to keep growing and flourishing. Whatever the season or economic climate throws at you.

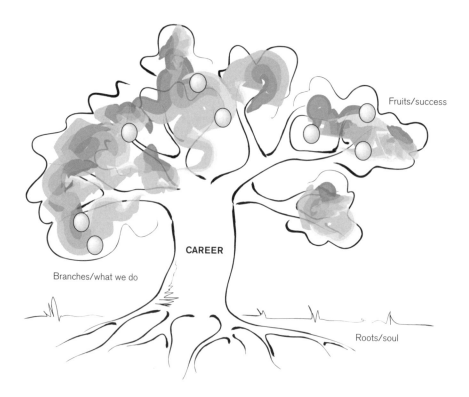

Fruits/success

CAREER

Branches/what we do

Roots/soul

Imagine the feeling of rootedness that will come from knowing who you are, and what you are aiming to achieve.

Life experiences are either about adding to or eroding your sense of personal completeness. Are you adding to or eroding your precious self this week? Soultrading is the process leading to happy authenticity – which might sound like a theory, but is actually a highly practical way of life. This brings me to the introductions. I'd like you to meet four people I know, all trying to wake up happier.

Soultrader – the stories

There are a few individuals trying to work out their best options using soultrader techniques. These are:

Jake Gold (Jake the Jaded)

Age 28, single, conference sound and lighting engineer
Hope = To carry on having a laugh and a drink
Current whiff of life purpose = 'You what, sorry?'

Emma McDonald (the star of Emma's Escape)

Age 25, married, two children, housewife
Hope = To study marketing
Current whiff of life purpose = 'To write adverts'

Claire Phillips (Life's Unfair Claire)

Age 33, single, banker
Hope = to be recognized for her financial talents
Current whiff of life purpose = 'To lead a major financial institution'

Steven Marksham (Straitjacket Steve)

Age 42 separated, three children, client relationship management (CRM) software salesman
Hope = Something less stressful, without losing out financially
Current whiff of life purpose = 'To build kids' confidence as a youth sports coach'

Jake the Jaded

Jake is an all-round top bloke.

Always first to the bar, last to depart. His friends can always rely on him for a last-minute favour. Nothing is ever too much trouble.

He owns a one-bed flat near the river and has plenty of 'company' but no one special in his life. Favourite films include *Reservoir Dogs* and (surprisingly) *Toy Story 2*. Which, after a few pints, become 'absolute classics'. In fact, Jake is at his best after at least a few pints, every night. Every single night.

Workwise, Jake is going great guns. He is the technical hub of a conference-organizing firm, the sound and vision man. Want some plasma screens in Milan for Tuesday morning? Call Jake. A live broadcast link from Manchester to Sydney next weekend, call Jake. He gets around 34k a year for this and loves it. Great team, great firm, lots of travel, nights out and a good laugh.

The only thing is, Jake isn't OK. He struts, but something just isn't wired for sound in his heart. He doesn't know what, and he feels it isn't anything to worry about, but he has got a sinking feeling. He feels he landed a great life by accident, and doesn't think he really deserves it. In Jake's secret thoughts lurks the expectation that one day, when he least expects it, the whole show will come down around his ears. *Game over*!

In the meantime, Jake's life rolls around one simple philosophy: if it's not going to kill you, it's not worth worrying about. Is it?

The story of Jake the Jaded

Do you know a Jake the Jaded? Do you think you could help? If so, what could you do? The answer is nothing, because he doesn't want help ... But he isn't entirely happy.

Another definition of happiness would be 'energized with purpose'.

So one way to tell if someone has wandered off their true path is their level of work/life energy or enthusiasm. If life feels a bit droopy and hard work, even after a good rest, it might be because of a purpose deficit. Now I am not suggesting this is happening to you, but it just might be. (Oh, and another thing, if this is happening to you, no one but you can make the changes. You make the changes in your life, no one else. Change is a door that can only be opened from the inside – a phrase I didn't invent, by the way).

Going back to Jake's story, he feels trapped, fearful, a bit lost. Yet he is, externally at least, doing really well. So how can he get back to the point where he feels right? Lets start by considering how Jake's disaffection with life came about.

Remember the earlier definition of soul as 'the vital animating force within'? Well, in each day you either add to that vital animating force or deplete it. Over time, a depleted soul means a defeated heart. Without energy, without joy, without optimism. Which is sort of where Jake seems to be. If Jake's soul has been depleted, what practical things can he do to change? Well first of all, the good news is that he *can* change.

It is possible to 'top up' the depleted soul, and you do that by regaining a sense of purpose. Because soul is most tangibly expressed as sense of purpose. Feeling energized with purpose is a litmus test.

Breaking this down into do-able practicalities, there are four main ingredients of this sense of purpose. Remember the soultrader tree – able to grow and flourish supported by four main roots? Those four roots again, are:

1 Experience (subdivided into the roots of knowledge, skills and attitude).

2 Learning (subdivided into the roots of risk taking and wonder).

3 Passion (subdivided into the roots of action, choice and change).

4 Trust (subdivided into the roots of expectation, patience and confidence).

We set up a chat with Jake to explore one of those roots, experience. What will this root, this ingredient of purpose, be able to tell him about what is going on with his working life?

Jake's roots experience	Questions	Jake's answers
	Jake, tell me about your career highs and lows so far.	The best bit was definitely getting this job, especially the first year when I was thrown in the deep end on all sorts of jobs and the travel and buzz was non-stop. That feels like a long time ago!
Experience sub-root: knowledge (defined as information and understanding)	What understanding did you bring to the job that you enjoyed using? Was it the technical side, or the client's needs? Has anything changed?	'It was the technical side of the job that appealed to me and got me into it — like getting two-way debate and electronic voting in three global sites, or getting a perfect sound mix in some aircraft hangar of a place. Blew the suits out of the water! The actual engineering is tricky, because you often get clients who want something completely impossible in the time. For example, one lot wanted a five-site satellite hub that same day. They think that just because they've got the money, they can get anything straight away. You get a lot of grief. We sorted them out five videoconferences — and even that was a complete nightmare. The technical side is as satisfying as hitting your head against a brick wall! The only good part is when it's over.
Experience sub-root: skills (defined as the ability to do something)	Jake, what kind of skills do you mostly use? Has this changed?	Well I still need to be on top of the science, but my job is being the gaffer, so the team know what has to happen and when. They often go to test before they've set up properly, and you run out of time. So I'm heavy Uncle Jake who stops mistakes. Which is a drag.
Experience sub-root: attitude (defined as temperament or approach)	What sort of attitude is needed to do this job? well?	The work is checking, rechecking — perfectionism. Then you tell the client what they want to hear to get them off your back. I suppose you need to encourage everyone along. And get people to pull their finger out. Especially Jason. He could twiddle for England.

What did you make of Jake's answers? It seemed helpful to ask him specific questions based on his experience, broken down into knowledge, skills and experience, rather than just saying 'You've turned into a misery, what's going on?'

His answers seem to suggest that the part of his job that made him happiest, the groovy science, has been replaced by team leadership, which he feels is a bit 'heavy'. Plus, as client-relationship manager, he spends more time talking to people he delightfully describes as 'the suits'. If it was the technical buzz and travel that was the high, and now he is the gaffer doing things that take him away from the most exciting and challenging part – making the technical theatrics work – then maybe it's no wonder he is a bit cheesed off. Wanting to take himself off site and into the boozer as soon as decently possible.

What do you think? What do you now think could be done to help Jake move on?

We won't go through all four roots right now, because we'll use those questions with some of the other characters. However, as you can see, asking the right questions gave us a chance to understand Jake's soul level dissatisfaction. So you know what's coming next.

Now I'm not for one moment suggesting you are Jake the Jaded's mirror image in the world. Just that you might want to look at how your 'vital, animating force' is doing at the moment.

Are you using your knowledge, skills and experience right now in a way that adds to or depletes your sense of purpose? If you have always wanted to use your marketing skills and you work as a PA, what is that doing to you? If you have lived abroad and speak fluent French and no one knows or cares, what is that doing to you? On the positive side, if you are turned on by ideas and blank sheets of paper and you are viewed as the creative whiz at work, what does that do for you? Good things right?

Use this exercise to evaluate those areas:

Am I using my experience to build purpose?

My roots: experience	Questions	My answers
	Tell me about your career highs and lows so far.	
Experience sub-root: knowledge (defined as information and understanding)	What understanding do you currently bring to your job? Is it technical or relationship, or a mixture?	
	What kind of information do you typically work with? Does this interest you, or would you prefer to work with other information, given a choice?	
Experience sub-root: skills (defined as the ability to do something)	What kind of skills do you mostly use? Are these the skills that you most want to use?	
	What do you want to change in terms of the skills you use most at work?	
Experience sub-root: attitude (defined as temperament or approach)	What sort of attitude is needed to do your current job well?	

Now, read those answers back. As you start to assemble data about your life, you might discover some ideas about what could improve. However, yours is only one view. There is a branch of psychology known as gestalt, which says that the whole is greater than the sum of its parts and encourages the individual to seek external perspective on events and perceptions, often through role play. For example, a gestalt intervention would be to imagine the part of you that feels upset by something at work sitting across from you in a chair, and to ask that separated-out part of you some questions. Another example is to ask yourself what your best friend would say to you in this situation.

Getting perspective is really important. So is the ability to shift your perspective, to understand what is happening in your life from another vantage point.

So after you have jotted down some responses to the questions above, look at your answers through the eyes of someone who cares about you. What would they say?

If you torture the data long enough, they will confess.
Massachusetts Institute of Technology (MIT) T-shirt

Given that, is there something you want to do differently? The root of your experience has got something to say about what is going on right now. What is it? What needs to happen so that you are happier, more fulfilled? You deserve happiness.

WHAT MAKES YOU HAPPY ABOUT YOUR WORK RIGHT NOW?

Being absolutely certain what I want to do and be and finding that I spend most of my time doing and being it or working towards doing and being it.

Sara Rowe, personal change trainer and coach, management consultancy

So just for yourself, for you to read and no one else, write down what you think needs to change.

Asking questions based on the root of your experience is one way to draw on the wisdom of your soul. If you ask better questions, chances are you'll get better answers. The roots of learning, passion and trust are resources to explore your most important career decisions in the same way.

Purpose

Aim, direction, aspiration, burning desire, intent, determination, expectation

Fulfilment

Accomplishment, achievement, completion, gratification, afterglow, realization

---

Let's look at where you are in your career right now. In your current job, do you feel engaged, productive and happy? Are you familiar with the idea of percentage utilization? Management consultants are big on this – it means the percentage of time being billed to clients. With apologies for the source of the lift, consider the percentage soul utilization going on in your job right now. How much root level nutrition gets up to your branches? Do you use your previous experience? Are you stimulated to learn and develop? Do you trust those around you and feel trusted? Do you feel passionate about what you are doing? If you are not hitting those, your career is not going to grow.

My shorthand for this is: do you feel your life has purpose? Before you close the page, feeling queasy at the thought of reading some deep Man's Quest for Meaning stuff, please be reassured. We are all finding this finding ourselves task hard. So I am going to try to be a straightforward no-jargon guide. Promise. The question is, are you bothered about being fulfilled or are you OK with life just being OK? There is no rule that says you have to feel happy, successful and fulfilled. If you are happy to wear your career like a pair of comfy slippers, that is fine, but expect to be embarrassed sometimes.

The soul of man is immortal and imperishable.

Plato (428–348 BC), *The Republic*

Fire and focus

If you know what your life purpose is, you will build a career around fulfilling it, give the whole experience 200 per cent, love it and therefore be more likely to succeed.

Is that it? Fine. Then I've got one more question.

How on earth am I meant to find my life purpose?

The purpose of our existence is to seek happiness.

His Holiness the Dalai Lama

It is never too late to be what you might have been.

George Eliot

Growing those ripe, luscious fruits of success requires that you first grow branches to sustain them. Those branches represent your career directions. This exercise is a chance for you to consider your current career direction, and state of growth, and maybe allow some truths to emerge.

For some time now, you might have been aware that you dream of something bigger, recognition of an expansive set of choices that are not present in reality. Daydreams create some natural justice, through expression, for our deepest, unvoiced aspirations.

I want you to invite the tingle of your own hopes nearer to the surface of your life, where you can feel them more deliciously. (Tingle, delicious? You sure? Yep. Delicious tingling works for me.)

In order to do that, it is important to find and write them down. Writing things down will make the process much easier, so that's why I really encourage you to take a few moments to get ready to do the exercise.

Most of all, don't worry about writing this for anyone but you. OK?

chapter one

soultrader

momentum

Fire

First of all write down about ten ideas off the top of your head on how you could set the world on fire. They don't all have to be about career – just let your imagination run wild. Don't censor on grounds of practicality, just connect with the flames of fame and fun for a moment. And don't worry about trying to prioritize them either just yet. It may take a while to get started. Maybe use these questions to help stimulate the flow …

- The audience thunders their applause. From centre-stage you look out at a sea of appreciative faces. You feel elated, delighted. What just happened?

- Close your eyes and see yourself being awarded the Nobel Prize. You are modest and succinct in victory. Why did you receive it?

- Your best friend phones up and says, 'Wow – I just read about you in the paper'. What did she/he just read about?

- You look at the letter containing your examination results and see the most amazing words. What are they?

- Over a new year's drink, you look back on the best year of your life. What was the best bit?

- You arrive in heaven and find your name with an entry next to it, summarizing the contribution you made to humanity while you were alive. What does it say?

Just to give you another few minutes to think, and maybe an example, here is my list. I could only do eight! Great role model already, eh?

How I'll set the world on fire. I will:

- Help people realize how gorgeous they are, and that they can take action.

- Get more people cycling and walking to reduce pollution.

- Write useful books.

- Create simple corporate social responsibility tools for business leaders.

- Expand the Magic Sandwich charity.

- Be a role model for a simple, happy life.

- Learn how to be a better coach and mentor.

- Write and engineer a perfect four-minute pop/dance track.

Now over to you. How are you going to set the world on fire?
This is how I'll set the world on fire. I will:

The brightest fire

The next part of the exercise is to rank these in terms of the tingle factor. Which of these do you really really want to make happen – which burn with a degree of intensity in your background thoughts? If none of the ideas cause you to tingle, then maybe you are not allowing yourself to write down the most secret, most desired hope. It is there, promise.

Rank your answers from one (the brightest fire), to ten (the least bright).

1

2

3

4

5

6

7

8

9

10

Now I didn't find it particularly easy to rank mine after about four or five. So if that happens, don't worry. Just get a sense of the most important ones.

Here are mine:

1 Help people realize how gorgeous they are, that they can take action.

2 Expand the Magic Sandwich charity.

3 Write useful books.

4 Be a role model for a simple, happy life.

5 Learn how to be a better coach and mentor.

6 Create corporate social responsibility tools for business leaders.

7 Write and engineer a perfect four-minute pop/dance track.

8 Get more people cycling and walking to reduce pollution.

The next part of the exercise is to work out what you will need to focus on to keep your life in smooth, easy-running order. These are the practical day-to-day providers of sanity.

Focus

What do you really have in your life? Do you need a certain amount of earnings or exercise? Do you have to keep learning and studying? Do you feel cramped without time on your own each week? Do you need to watch the whole nine-hour *Eastenders* omnibus? Some things we need more than others.

Your choices indicate some values. Values are a form of footprint from the soul – they are the visible part of what's below. Now some people feel values have a must-be-lovely connotation. Not so. Values are neutral. Your values are your values and you are entitled to say what is important to you and not feel you have to act in a certain way. If your values are to get the car and the house, then fine, great. Acknowledge that and you'll be less stressed sitting in local community meetings talking about how to listen to issues. Maybe because after reading this you won't be there!

It's too easy to sit in a nice, well-paid job in some government quango losing your natural 'action man' self. For goodness sake, leave your desk, get out there and do it. Be a policeman, be a fireman, be a hero! Don't wimp on about how the family wants you to stay. Just be true to yourself and say what is most important to you, without an audience of all the people in your life. Sitting at that desk watching your hopes fade isn't what you deserve. Trust your instinct on this – if you get going on the right path, even if it doesn't end up exactly where you'd planned, it'll still be better than being part of the view from the door to the fourth floor. Or wherever you are.

Focus: this is important to me

Consider these questions. Imagine all your essential needs are met, and you are asked to pick a small number of important but not live-or-die items. You line up to be allocated a daily ration, choosing five from the following. What do you choose? Just give this your gut feel – which of these choices sound most you?

Time with your loved ones (partner, parents, children)	
Extra £100	
Facial, manicure, pedicure	
Exercise	
Time to cook proper food	

►

Time to paint, draw, compose – to create in some way	
Travel	
Work on your new project	
Latest computer	
Time listening to music	
Time walking along the seafront or woods (anywhere natural and peaceful)	
Socializing time with friends	
Clubbing	
Time alone	
Time to read, study or learn	
Intimacy	
Work using my skills and experience (which pays well enough to enjoy life)	
Sunshine	
Extra sleep	
Shopping	
Alcohol	

Here are mine:

Time with your loved ones (partner, parents, children)	Yes
Extra £100	
Facial, manicure, pedicure	
Exercise	
Time to cook proper food	
Time to paint, draw, compose – to create in some way	
Travel	
Work on your new project	
Latest computer	
Time listening to music	Yes
Time walking along the seafront or woods (anywhere natural and peaceful)	Yes

Socializing time with friends	
Clubbing	
Time alone	
Time to read, study or learn	
Intimacy	Yes
Work using my skills and experience (which pays well enough to enjoy life)	Yes
Extra sleep	
Shopping	
Alcohol	

Now over to you – why not write down all the things that you do (look in your diary for inspiration) and then choose just five.

The things that you choose here, as part of your day, are also a summary of the most important things in your life. Now try to put them in order of priority.

My top five focus

1
2
3
4
5

Now we bring the two exercises together.

In this continued spirit of honesty, here is my combined fire and focus.

Top five fire (what I really, really want to do)	Top five focus (what has to be in my life to keep me sane and solvent)
1 Help people realize how gorgeous they are so that they can take action.	**1** Time with loved ones (partner, parents, children).
2 Expand the Magic Sandwich charity until we know there are no hungry schoolchildren.	**2** Time listening to music.
3 Write useful books to pass on what I have learned and am learning.	**3** Time walking along the seafront or woods (anywhere natural and peaceful).
4 Be a role model for a simple, happy life.	**4** Work using my skills and experience (which pays well enough to enjoy life).
5 Write the perfect four-minute single.	**5** Intimacy.

And now over to you (sorry about all this rewriting – at least you get to decide how true your choices are at each stage!).

My combined fire and focus list

Top five fire	Top five focus
1	**1**
2	**2**
3	**3**
4	**4**
5	**5**

Hopefully, this exercise is helping you rank these choices, which you may not have been aware of. The hopes you have of setting the world on fire, combined with the practicality of day-to-day life, are rarely combined on the same page. We hop between the two, mentally, hoping that some communality will spring out from somewhere.

The commute from what seems practical and what is most desirable can be quite stressful. For a long time, I held back from what I most wanted to do (help get food to hungry children in London) because I thought that the only way to do it would be full time, back to penury, and 100 hours a week, thereby sending my so-far happy relationship to the bottom of the list of things to do every day. So I thought about it, and thought about it, and eventually found a way to work on something small, which is better than nothing, and allows me to contribute something. The result was more energy, in a way that I couldn't have predicted. I feel strongly that this is because the thing I'm doing is right for me.

It is possible to take tiny, baby steps to fulfilment, and stay in control. It isn't all or nothing.

When you look at the top scores for fire, and the top scores for focus, you realize that your life does have some priorities. Look at the list. Are you sure they are right? Is there anything else you might have forgotten, coming up on the inside lane, as it were? OK. Now I want you to map these on to a model that brings together the fire and focus priorities.

First, start with the answers you marked four or five. Write your fire choices on the left side, your focus choices on the right. They should lie within the bottom left arch. Then your answers marked two and three. Again, write your fire choices on the left side, your focus choices on the right. They should lie within the middle band. Finally, the answers you marked as number one. Fire on the left, focus on the right. These answers should appear in the top right-hand corner. You should now see a prioritized model.

high fire + high focus = your purpose

Fire and focus model
To identify your life priorities

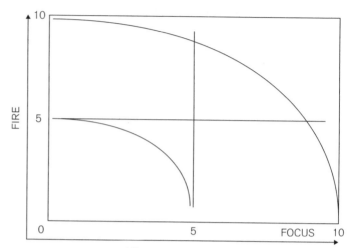

What am I passionate about?

Use the vertical axis to rank your life's desire.

FIRE

FOCUS

What are the things you really want/need to do?

Your high-fire list might be very different to your high-focus list – in which case that in itself indicates that your life is constructed around activities that do not motivate to the highest possible degree. So no wonder you aren't burning with enthusiasm most days. If you have got some overlap between the two, great. Those are the areas to expand.

The answers that make their way into the top right-hand corner are the building blocks of your life purpose.

If your soul could indicate a way forward in your life, it would be a pathway using the intentions you have just identified.

I want to emphasize that this is a starting place, a way to question assumptions. What happens next is up to you. What did you experience emotionally in writing out those ideas? Did you start to warm up, get into it? Did it make you feel a bit sad, like some sense of loss? Did you have to blank out and get some tea or a toasted peanut butter and banana sandwich?

If your life isn't perfect right now, remember the soultrader core concepts. You are gorgeous, gifted and unique, and you are capable of making all the right decisions in your life. No one has a perfect life. No one has a perfect job. Supermodels speak of the tyranny of diets and dull shoots. Oh God, the Maldives again.

What do the experts say?

People Management (24 August 2001) reported on research concerning the career hopes of 1681 14-year-olds. Stephen Gauntlet, one of the report authors and chief executive of Sussex Careers Centre, said: 'The most important factor when considering a career was that it be "a job that interests me" followed by "pay" and then "time for interests outside work".'

He also commented: 'Five to ten years ago, people were looking for power. Now they are looking for fulfilment.'

Source: Roffey Park Management Institute and Sussex Careers Service, 2000 survey of 40 schools

It might be useful to think about the life you are in right now as the transition to more fulfilment, more alignment with the things that are important. You are letting those priorities unfold. You are doing a good job and it is getting better. Can you allow yourself to think that?

Please remember that your thoughts create your life. What's in your head right now is the script for what happens tomorrow.

So take this exercise as a start. If you noticed frustration with your current situation creeping in, that's fine. I once read that we wouldn't have pearls if it weren't for oysters getting irritated (sorry, I accept your right-minded rejection of all cheesy metaphors). The point is, it really is possible to find your life purpose by asking the right questions and allowing some time to unearth the true story of you. It is time to get excited and passionate about your life.

I (also) can't understand people that aren't passionate about something. The world is too fantastic a place not to be motivated by some cause/idea/whim – everyone has their difference to make and people that fail to even try just leave me cold. I often feel damming about this: VS Naipaul hit it on the head in *A Bend in the River*, 'The world is what it is. Those who are nothing, who allow themselves to become nothing, have no place in it'.

John Marchant, founder of business 360.com

Does life purpose and soul hold any real interest to ordinary people, in a fast-paced, profit-minded global market? Well that depends on a number of things. For example, if your current job is not giving you the chance to learn and develop new skills, would that be a problem? According to a survey on the momentum website,[1] the chance to learn is a high priority, followed closely by an answer that seems very close to the question of soul, purpose and identity.

The 'what do we want from work?' survey

What is your main goal in your current job? job?	Percentage (of those who answered)	1 = most common response
To earn as much as possible	8%	3
To learn and develop new skills	**54%**	**1**
To find out more about myself and what I'm made of	27%	2
To get promoted	4%	4
To survive until next year	8%	3

[1] (31 people completed the survey during September/October 2001: 44 per cent were male respondents, 56 per cent were female; most respondents were UK based, with one respondent from each of Hong Kong, Zambia, Australia, Canada, France and the Netherlands).

There is a consistent theme (it is acknowledged, of course, that there is respondent bias because the survey is within a website showcase for career development). Here is a selection of responses to the question, 'How is your current work good for your soul?'

'It gives me an additional purpose in life, it is something that I have a passion about, I work with some excellent people, I am having fun, I am learning.'

'I have worked out my core purpose. When I am working to purpose I am able to work at peak energy. I am at a major change crossroads so I am still doing some work I may choose to dump later. But I know where I am headed.'

Do you believe your current work is good for your soul?

'No (but how I act is, regardless of work or non-work situations).'

'I am honouring the fact that I cannot work for anyone, or any institution any longer that does not have the same work ethic and relationship values that I do. I am also trusting that who I am is enough, and that my work has to come from my heart and with integrity.'

'It is my work – it is creative, about supporting others in new ways of working. It is contributing to the wider world at a number of levels – directly to clients, indirectly by raising the level of discussion and awareness of emotional issues and new ways of working.'

What has been your most effective career strategy so far?	Percentage (of those who answered)	1 = most common response
Knowing the right people	7%	5
Getting the right qualifications	7%	5
Choosing work that I really enjoy	22%	2
Being in the right place at the right time	8%	4

Proving I can do a good job, and getting noticed	41%	1
Having a career/life balance	19%	3
Office politics skills	0%	6

Does your current job:	Percentage (of those who answered)	1 = most common response
Feed your body?	32%	2
Feed your soul?	0%	4
Both?	43%	1
Neither?	25%	3

A high number of the responses indicated a desire to do fulfilling work – as you would expect. It is worth noting that a quarter of respondents feel both unfulfilled and impoverished by work.

What would Zorro do?

Homer Simpson, *The Simpsons*

PRACTICAL SOULSEARCHING

Is there anything you currently do that causes you to become so engrossed that lunchtime is a complete surprise?

Energized with purpose

Think again of your high-fire, high-focus priorities. What did you decide the root of your experience was telling you? Did you identify anything to improve? 'If I change this, will it make me happy?'

If you have listed parts of your working life that need to change, I have one quick question for you. If all those things were to change, every one of them, would you be happy then? Really. OK. Now we'll take each of those priorities and walk them through your preferred method of change. What does that mean? It is essential to attempt to live a life that is closer to your purpose (start soultrading) using a learning style that is right for you.

If you are an activist, you'll have to try stuff out and fall over and get up and fall over and learn that way. If you are a reflector, you will need to do some analysis. If you are a pragmatist, you'll look for the connections between this exercise and others you have tried. If you are a theorist, you will want to consider the concepts in more detail. For more on this, take a look at the learning cycle by Honey and Mumford (*Manual of Learning Styles*, 1992).

◆ Figure out what is most important and practically achievable.

◆ Work out your preferred learning style.

◆ Get an external conscience (a friend) to talk through your ideas.

◆ Identify something from the high-fire, high-focus list that you feel can be achieved.

◆ Do it.

◆ Review what happened and keep going.

Being energized with purpose is the ultimate motivator.

chapter two
working a way to your soul

Is it possible to simply add more fulfilment to your working life? The answer is yes, and this chapter shows how.

Your life. Don't be plastic about it.

We can do better than inhabit global blands.

Wouldn't it be nice to have the courage to stand up, stand out, and be different? The soultrader is bespoke, able to thrive off the beaten track and feel good about an achievement for its own sake. Trained to be appraised, as we are, we expect each achievement to merit external applause. When was the last time you felt great inside without having to tell everyone about it? The process of becoming happy, fulfilled and successful is not something you are necessarily going to get external applause for.

So it is important to be able to sustain yourself as you become more authentic, more energized with purpose.

Every soul is a melody which needs renewing.

Stéphane Mallarmé (1842–1898), French symbolist poet

This matters; an approval habit is expensive to maintain.

An unfettered approval habit can turn you into the firm's equivalent of the dancing bear. Before you know it, everything is so the boss will say well done. Not about your soul's wellbeing. Over time, it is easy to grow a plastic soul and end up as a plastic person, singing for the firm's salary, your manager's smile.

48% of 4126 male executives saw their lives as empty and meaningless, despite years of professional striving.

George Lemay, Association of Humanistic Psychology, 1989

Dangerously, you forget what is most important to you. The boss wants the report Monday so you have to work Sunday. Sorry kids, daddy can't go to the cinema. As a plastic person, you forget to explore your potential until retirement (given that evenings and weekends are so busy). You don't care as long as the job gives you that approval fix.

Isn't it possible you deserve a chance to experience yourself in the most authentic way possible? To 'do who you are' and then decide, from that place of awareness, where best to pour your valuable attention.

authenticity = personal brand integrity = competitive and financial advantage

Jobs are increasingly perishable items, so isn't it a better strategy to do what you really want to do?

Perhaps it is more effective, and healthy, to aim your talents at fulfilling work, rather than a job where the main benefit is being told you are doing OK? You can do that for yourself and get on with something more important.

Trapped by lack?

What about the idea that you can only enjoy the luxury of happiness and fulfilment after you get rich? Do you believe that only the rich are able to choose meaningful work? Or another angle – do you feel you deserve lots of money? There can be a pretty self-sabotaging double whammy on this: 'I'm never going to make more than enough money to survive on, and only the people with big bank accounts get to be creative and happy.' Thoughts like that can create a boundary between you and a career enriched with purpose.

Your career can be energized with purpose wherever you are on the local pay scale. Equally you can be Mr or Ms victim and decide life has to be nasty, brutish and short, even if you earn ten grand a day. Your thinking is the difference. The soultrader acknowledges personal responsibility for earning capacity and grows the confidence to steer towards work that feels right, that animates. Profit tends to be the by-product of great products or services. So find where your self is most energized – that's likely to be where your fortune lies.

This isn't fairy-tale stuff. There is a virtuous circle of I believe I can have work that is sustaining and right for me; I believe that role will be the best way for me to really give 100 per cent and succeed.

You and I are responsible for our financial wellbeing and happiness. So to identify what might be happening in your thoughts and in your life around finances, it might be useful to go back to the soultrader roots exercise (remember how the roots of experience, learning, passion and trust are visible expressions of life purpose) to help assess the roots of your financial purpose.

Financial purpose

What do the roots of my experience say about money and me?

E.g. access to finance, my habits, my attitude:

- ◆ In the past
- ◆ Right now
- ◆ In the future?

What does the root of my passion say about me and money?

- ◆ What must I have?
- ◆ What attracts me to or puts me off financial success?
- ◆ What are my passionate extravagances?

What does the root of my trust say about money and me?

- ◆ Do I expect my future to include financial success?
- ◆ What is my earnings range now and in five years time?
- ◆ Do I have a self-imposed earnings limit?
- ◆ What are my family views?

What does the root of my learning say about me and money?

- ◆ How do I rate in terms of financial awareness – honestly?
- ◆ Could I become clued up about saving and investment?
- ◆ Could I learn to take financial control of my life?

There is no prescriptive agenda here – there is no question of a generic right level of earning. I would just like to suggest that you have the power to trap or liberate your earnings potential. As a financially confident soultrader, you will have space to make better career choices. Equally, better career choices give financial rewards.

Can I continue with this idea of asking better questions to get better career outcomes? The questions and answers below point to the difference a mindset can make:

	Question	Soul-level frustration might show up in your thoughts as follows	Some alternative (soultrader) thoughts
1	What am I doing with my life?	• I'm [insert age] and I still don't know what I want to do when I grow up • I'm bored. • Why does everyone else get all the sexy jobs?	• I can steer this career based on what is really important to me. • I achieve my own definition of success. • People here want me to succeed and be happy.
2	Am I good enough?	• I'm no good at anything I really want to do. • I'm not clever at maths (or spelling, or languages, or whatever). • I feel like a fraud. • I didn't get promoted so I must be useless. • Why can't I speak up for myself?	• I'm going to give it a go. • Whatever happens, I'm learning and out there. • I trust that I can do whatever I really want to do. Look how far I have come already! • I am realistic about what I can do and what I really want to do, and set myself realistic targets.
3	How can I tell if this is the right career for me?	• This is a career that started by accident – I'm not sure it ever it felt right. • No one believes this is what I really want to do for a living. • This isn't what I want to be doing in five years' time. • I am always so tired. • I'm looking elsewhere.	• I know where I'm going. • I only take that feels right and satisfying. • I can say no to work that takes me away from where I want to be. • I can be free agent, even if I stay here with the firm.
4	Can I change my job to something that interests me more?	• This isn't so bad: at least the people are nice. • Good jobs have crap pay and I need money. • Look at the economy – not a • good time to change. • My family, friends, colleagues, and cat want me to stay.	• I am in control of my career. • I can go after my ideal, and it will be OK. • Happiness comes first. • Money will come from something I can really put everything into. • My career path is mine to walk down. And mine to sit by the side of when I need to. My choice.

Soulskimming

Lets look at the opposite of soultrading: soulskimming. Skimming through each big life event, ever so slightly wanting it to be over. What's next? Soulskimming is not daring to do it properly now in case you get it wrong, buying skimmed milk because you ought to and hating every drop, putting the thing you most want to do at number 11 on a list of ten.

Soulskimmers wait until they feel better placed to enjoy all the soft fruit of a happy life. It isn't going to happen. Believe me. As a soulskimmer you'll stand on stage, with an adoring crowd, and find yourself vaguely wondering how you'll get home afterwards. You'll kiss the being of your dreams but forget to wake up until it's over.

Your soul waits and asks 'Shall I put some tea on, for when you get here?'

Soulskimmers live on the surface of life's rich opportunities. For reasons that include fear, lack of formal training in life's little knocks and minimal experience in just being happy. I skim less these days, but I do. What's your skim rate?

Might you be having a quiet skim right here and now?

My full, semi-skimmed or skimmed life – a test

Answer a, b or c to the following:

1 You work hard for days to get a report done. The boss comes over and starts to say, 'Marion, this is great.' Ignoring the fact that your name is Wendy. What is your most normal reaction?
   a) Start humming a little tune in your head and look down until he goes away.
   b) Look him in the eyes and smile warmly to let him know you are glad to be recognized for the hard work.
   c) Stand up, spill coffee on the desk and mutter 'It was nothing,' while mopping frantically.

2 Your team gets the chance to present at the annual leadership event. You decide to:
   a) Have flu that week.
   b) Get the team together to work on the piece, ahead of time.
   c) Ignore it until one week before, then panic and put together something painfully stressful for the day.

3 At your best friend's housewarming party, do you:
   a) Create a private space and read his old *GQ* magazines?
   b) Get to know what is happening in the lives of your old friends?
   c) Get drunk, fall into the faux fireplace and cause the planned DIY/repair weekend to happen a month early?

4 When reading an article about your specialist field of work, do you:
   a) Think, blimey I could have written that, then forget it immediately?
   b) Note the e-mail and invite the author to lunch to compare approaches?
   c) Add a handlebar 'tache and pointy ears to her photo?

If you answered mostly a

You are a probably an introvert skimmer, creating as little fuss as possible, yet probably wanting to achieve huge amounts. Your need to stay in your comfort zone is growing by the day. The soultrader response is to think that all your fear doesn't actually exist in the world outside your head. The question is, when do you plan to take the brakes off your journey to success by first realizing you do a great job, and your friends love you?

If you answered mostly b

You come across as someone who wants to live in the moment and enjoy it. This is great – and you don't need anyone to tell you. Make sure you also help those who are not as clued in as you. The sin of smugness is the worst one.

If you answered mostly c

Apart from being an extrovert skimmer, you are potentially on a collision course for the rest of your life! The energy you burn at the point of someone calmly congratulating you could resurrect a dark star. The goal would be to have a day or two with the phrase 'I like who I am' in the back of your mind.

Soulskimming. What am I going to wear? Background drone of next year, last year, same as it ever was, same as it ever was. Put the kettle and the radio on. Try to get out the door by 8am. Talking Heads, letting the days go by. Nearly 7.40am. Listening to the breakfast show with the same cereal, same shoes, same website to choose. 7.55am. I don't mind. Easy day today. Not having a bad year. I haven't got a bad life really. Soulskimming. Have I had a once-in-a-lifetime experience yet? Clock says ten past. Ten years past …

Reduce your skim rate

Potential skim event	What you could do instead
Your appraisal.	You remember when. You prepare. You make sure the boss knows what you have done. You say what you want to do next.
Your next job.	You hear about it. You phone straight away. You find out what they want and you send a letter today, saying how you want to help. You expect to get it. You research. You tell them how they'll benefit from hiring you in the interview. You get the job.
Chance to tell the boss's boss your ideas. Can you be bothered?	Your boss's boss is always looking for good ideas, and you've got one. They were once where you are. You tell them.
Your redundancy.	They are going to downsize your department. You phone HR and arrange an early chat. You do your home finances – how much do you need each month – and assess your marketable skills. You figure a time to go, with three months' jobsearch. You see HR, suggest a leaving date, and negotiate some retraining. They agree, seem helpful. No one else has talked to them. It's hard, but you're calling the shots.

Potential skim event	What you could do instead
Do-nothing days followed by major guilt, whizzing through without as much care as should be there.	You have worked out what you want to make happen. And day-to-day priorities feel reasonably clear. So though you can't always get them all done, you are mostly pleased with progress.
You can't remember what happens next career wise.	You keep talking to people and testing ideas about what might open up next. You keep an open mind on being successful at this or something else that feels right.
Your life.	You are emotionally and mentally, as well as physically, present while it happens.

Skimmers have a habit of skimming. It becomes normal, easy. This is who I am. I skim. That's it.

The wake-up call from your soul can help. Remembering that your purpose is to be happy, fulfilled and successful is a good start. When the Buddha was asked what was different after he found enlightenment, he replied, ' I am awake.'

Kick the skim habit

Might it help to forward-plan your next month to kick the skim habit? OK. What we need to do is find out the next significant event, (e.g. a presentation, appraisal, interview, client meeting or whatever it is that you are dreading – you know what it is). Get out your diary and write the following. It can also apply to the big date/family event/parent evening …

Today's date

Significant events coming up this week

Next week

Next month

On each one there is a skim option:

◆ Forget all about it.

◆ Have a major last-minute panic.

◆ Try bluffing on the day.

◆ Suffer post-event regret, low self-esteem and punishing of
  anything in range, e.g. dogs or small children.

◆ The brain will try to forget the next time (and ladies and,
  gentlemen, a pattern is born!).

Does that sound familiar? Take a look at this week. Are you planning
to give that number-one event a good, big skim? OK – fine, we all do
it. And while these patterns don't change overnight, your desire to
improve things for yourself is something you can do in an instant. A
millisecond now could put something quite amazing in motion. Really.

You see life always offers choice. Wow – here come the one million
reasons why you have virtually no choice! I can hear them from right
the way over here. Life always offers choice. The presence of free will
is about the only phrase I agree with from my early years as a nice
Catholic girl.

You have choices, you can choose the option most likely to lead to
happiness, success and fulfilment – the opposite of the soulskim
option. Right now. All you have to do is look at the significant events

in your diary. You have a choice to look in your diary now or just say forget it, can't be bothered … happy here.

Against each one, you:

◆ Check it out in advance.

◆ Figure out the desired outcome.

◆ Be awake and alert during the event.

◆ Record some of the things you get from it.

◆ And follow through.

What language do you naturally think in – soulalert or soulskim? Take one event in one week and find out what a big difference this choice will make.

Awakening to purpose significantly increases your chances of success – creating meaningful, inspiring, nutritious work.

That's all on skimming for now.

Next up is Claire, a young woman about to discover the career value of thought.

Life's Unfair Claire goes for promotion

Claire works for a large retail bank in the finance division. She joined aged 23 as a part-qualified accountant and has stayed ever since. At the moment, she is team leader for a group of six financial controllers, working in the settlements area. Claire is hardworking and ambitious – she sees this job as a stepping stone to a strategic finance role. In terms of attitude and personality, she is a strong character, keen to make her point in

Anyway, Andy, the mild-mannered head of department, has decided to leave. Claire has been one of five people working directly for Andy for two years, with good feedback on her team. She reckons hers to be closest to his way of thinking.

Before the interview

Claire applies and gets selected for interview. The night before, she makes an inventory of wins and notes down some examples of her leadership style. As with all effective interviewees, Claire soundbites well. She can count on winners like the top three benefits of customer-driven technology. And her key project experience will sound impressive.

We join Claire at about 9.15pm the night before, at a location inside her head.

'I imagine Euan will be on the panel, bless him, from HR. Couldn't manage his way out of a paper bag. Mmm, does he remember the time I told his secretary that he shouldn't overdo it, staying until 5.50pm? What is he going to say when I get the job? As if they'd ever let me really sort them out! Anyway, if I don't get the job, I'll know they've fixed it. And I won't stay. No way.'

What happens

Claire interviewed well. Came across as professional, clear and competent. Her answers were very well structured and the data helpful. Only one thing concerned the panel. When asked about the senior team (at the next management level), she wasn't particularly complementary. Surely (thought the collective mind of the panel) any new appointee would need to work effectively as part of the team. Apart from that, Claire was a very impressive candidate. But, just as she thought, the job went to someone else, someone less adept financially perhaps, but an instinctive communicator and aligned personal-style-wise with senior management. Claire hears the news, decides that once again she has been the best candidate but her face didn't fit. 'I'm not surprised, to be honest. Life's so unfair, isn't it?'

Eventually, everyone sits down to a banquet of consequences.

Robert Louis Stevenson

It would be good to help Claire figure out what has happened. Remember this isn't the first time.

One way to tell if someone has lost their sense of purpose is the fact that they have low expectation of success. They have lost hope in the happy ending. Claire sees life as a fixed match. The outcome is always Life 2, Claire 0. This is called scarcity mentality – there isn't enough success, fairness, money or friends, and you are not going to ever get enough and that's just how it is because life's unfair. You have probably known people like that. People who couldn't ever have enough and whatever they did felt as if it could be taken away from them at any time. Scarcity merchants.

Remember the earlier definition of soul as the vital animating force within? If Life's Unfair Claire has lost hope, if she has got a scarcity mentality, then perhaps what's needed is a soul level injection. What practical things can she do to change?

Once again, soul is most tangibly expressed as sense of purpose, and there are four main ingredients of purpose. The four roots are:

1 Experience (subdivided into the roots of knowledge, skills and attitude).

2 Learning (subdivided into the roots of risk taking and wonder).

3 Passion (subdivided into the roots of action, choice and change).

4 Trust (subdivided into the roots of expectation and patience).

We've already looked at the first one when we asked Jake the Jaded some questions to assess what the root of his experience could tell him. Now let's ask Claire about the roots of her learning. She is, post-rejection letter, still trying to work it all out. Not feeling that good in herself.

Claire's roots of learning	Questions	Claire's answers
	Claire, tell me about your career highs and lows so far.	Well right now the highs are hard to think about. I've just had some bad news about the promotion that had my name on it. Or so I thought. So think this is as low as I've been. I feel I have worked so hard for this bank and got almost nothing back. Time to do something different. Um. Sorry, but I'm not in any mood to think of highs.
Learning sub-root: risk taking	Did this job experience feel outside your comfort zone?	Not really. It felt like more of the same. More taken for granted. More hard work but don't expect much.
	So what would be outside your comfort zone?	That's easy [laughs]. Life treating me fairly for once. Not that that's going to happen.
Learning sub-root: wonder	OK. Tell me about things you really enjoy. What makes you feel like a child – overawed with wonder?	That's a hard one. The last time that happened I was on holiday, on a boat, and I saw a kingfisher come down with turquoise wings and pull a silver fish from the river. That was amazing.
Claire's roots of learning	Questions	Claire's answers
	Wasn't it amazing that you should be in the right place at the right time to see it?	I was incredibly lucky. That one time. It'll probably never happen again.

It was a short conversation – Claire wasn't in the mood. The roots of her learning reinforce the idea that life is cruel and hard, and so the experience keeps repeating. Scarcity mentality can cause life to feel like an unrelenting struggle, with some new loss just round the corner.

The frustrating thing is that no matter how many times someone says, 'You are going to get what you expect to get,' it has to hit home in the gut to register properly. We create the outcomes that we believe are most likely to happen. So I can't help but think that leaving won't change the record inside Life's Unfair Claire. Every firm will be like the bank, full of denigrators, conspiracies, lazy so and so's, unless she experiences life as abundant, full of ways to succeed, until she genuinely feels a sense of wonder and excitement about the things she can achieve.

The kingfisher moment has stayed in her memory, so there is a suggestion of brilliance, of life having spectacular moments. That small moment could be the spark to help the rest of her confidence catch fire. The shift from scarcity to abundance can come from understanding that our natural world has huge abundance. Our soultrader tree doesn't hang on to leaves, it lets go because next spring there will be thousands of buds ready to open out their fresh green selves. Our soultrader branches don't stay rigid thinking, 'Right, I've grown 15 twigs and that's my lot!' They keep growing and flourishing as long as the environment has enough nutrition.

Your environment has more than enough nutrition for your soul. Your workplace has more than enough challenges for you to get involved with and learn; there is a world full of causes, adventures, and new stuff just waiting to be tried. Your colleagues want to support you, want to make things work. Your skills and talents have the ability to become products and services that could make you more money than you have ever dreamed of. We live in abundance, but sometimes our thoughts live in scarcity. Luckily, we can choose to change.

Life's Unfair Claire has retreated from her environment as a result of her scarcity mentality, and it is hurting her more than anyone.

Scarcity thinking is a habit and we all build up patterns of behaviour. That's normal. The ability to learn, to expect things to work out, to be awake and alert is a soultrader strategy. Behavioural psychologists know lots of bigger and, maybe, better words for pretty much the same thing. Decide to learn to be happy.

There are two main lessons from Life's Unfair Claire at this stage. First is that her happiness, success and fulfilment are being jeopardized by her scarcity thinking. Second, she doesn't seem to realize that the same thinking gives the same outcomes; instead, she blames the latest unfair situation.

It can be career limiting to do something (this week) believing it to be the very first time it happened, when in fact it always happens. We forget, repeat, get the same results, think this is life when actually it is just one script.

In our careers, we get what we think we'll get. What do you think you deserve?

Directing the traffic of thoughts inside your head directs the passage of events through the next 50 years or so. On a personal note, can I just say that once that bit of information took hold as a belief, my life was transformed. I was Life's Unfair Claire. Oh yes. My life's unfair mantra included 'Rich people always get everything', and 'Us women never get a chance', 'My family are just unlucky'. Those scarcity thoughts made me feel hopeless, depressed. What's the point of giving something your all if life is going to present itself as a size 10 boot in your face every time? My roots were in trouble.

It is really hard to get into life purpose and fulfilment if your life just about hangs together on a very thin, stressed thread day to day. It is essential to sort out the basics before heading on – call me an old Maslovian but the hierarchy of needs really applies here.

Practically speaking, that means security, a sense of belonging and self-esteem. No problem there then! Aren't we all working on self-esteem on this journey? I know I am.

soultrader

momentum

There are some other basics to address. First of all is the ability to be the priority in your life. No way to avoid this one – if your whole world is putting everyone else first to the point of ignoring your own needs, then that is first up (there are some great ideas on this in *Coach Yourself*, Grant and Greene, momentum, 2001). Put yourself first and get some time to reflect – you need room to breathe. One test is this: in any given week, are you able to listen to some of your favourite music? Are you able to read the newspaper for more than five minutes without interruption? Are you?

Take a music bath once or twice a week for a few seasons, and you will find that it is to the soul what the water bath is to the body.

Oliver Wendell Holmes Jr (1809–1894)

The second basic to get in place is the emotional and financial support network. Being trapped in a hard relationship or in debt is a hard place to start discovering your life's purpose. It isn't impossible – but way better to line up your friends, family and workmates as allies before you start asking the big questions. Hang on, I hear you say, don't we assume life lacks emotional support and financial freedom? Isn't that why we need *Soultrader*?

If you are reading this in debt, in pain, with psychological or physical difficulties that frame your life in a particularly difficult way, the soultrader guide might frustrate. Soultrading is the best personal career strategy for sustainable career success, building on your act being sufficiently together to make steps forward.

That is exactly what I had to do. In 1989, my life was a seriously serial crisis. How did I get out of it? Three ways: first, I listened to people who suggested that I might enjoy life more if I sorted out the constant sources of high stress (sounds strangely simple but it really worked). I started paying off long-term debts slowly, reduced my spending, helped my sister find a lovely place to live, which reduced her day-to-day grief (and mine), decided to go for a swim once or twice a week, and began to feel better about myself.

Slowly I got out of debt and the 25-hour day that debt brings. I began to feel like part of the normal working world again. I will always remember the first lunchtime at work when I could just go for a sandwich, like everyone else, and not be on the payphone desperately staving off today's imminent disaster. Good grief! For a couple of years I felt the rest of my life was going to be talking the bailiffs out of putting the telly in their van and driving off. With that kind of fundamental stress there was no way I could think about an inspiring career! If you are there, please contact me* and I can put you in touch with a bunch of good resources – there is an infrastructure to support you even if you feel there is nothing good in your life.

Second, I got lucky. One dull job (secretary, telecom firm, note-taker at waffly, losing-the-will-to-live meetings – you get the picture) contained the lucky bonus of an encouraging boss and an unrestricted job description. I was encouraged to learn, to use my talents, and I enjoyed myself so much I forgot to be oppressed. Without realizing, the act of achieving a few small challenges pulled me into a new mindset. I forgot life was all meant to go wrong.

Third, with this new-found courage, I started to study, started to learn about the job, the firm and the marketplace, to the point where work was more than slogging through an in-tray to put money in my bank account. It became an interesting problem to be solved, it became a set of friends with ideas on how to solve it.

The most important working environment turned out to be the one inside my skull.

* carmelmcconnell@hotmail.com

Stopping soul sabotage

If you have Life's Unfair Claire tendencies, try this:

During one day, catch the phrases you use about yourself. It might be 'I'm so crap at numbers'. It might be 'Typical, it doesn't work' or 'I don't deserve that'. Write down at least five.

Next to them write the opposite. Now each time your 'Life's Unfair Claire' thought pops up, just say, 'I can do this' or 'I am in control of this, and I can choose the right direction'. Use words that work for you.

Here is an example. I found that it was a real habit for me to lose important information or my keys or my purse. I'd get in my car without a map, etc. So I'd be saying, 'Bet I've lost it' to myself at least a million times a day. Which of course kept the idea fresh in my mind, so I'd keep repeating the pattern. Now at the back of my diary is: 'I handle important information carefully.'

I know it sounds far fetched but the simple act of saying encouraging, gentle things to yourself rather than constantly having a go is a quantum step forward. So think about your top phrases. Then their opposites. Then say the opposite as much as you can. Try it for one day. Yes, it feels weird. Our brains work like computers, literally on instructions, so we need better innerware to operate them. This is the first step to reduce soul-level self-sabotage.

The conversation with Claire and the exercise above can hopefully help you to see that you could be blindsided on the way you do life. Are you open to it being good and easy, or open to it being mean and hard? Remember you really only have two career choices to make at any time. Do you see yourself leaving your current job or staying?

Will you leave quiet and hurt or loud and dramatic? Will you stay and allow good things to happen? Claire could get to age 60 thinking her whole life will feel unfair unless she gets hold of her thinking and turns it around. And it is just the same for you and I.

Here's one. You come home from work and the heating is broken. Faced with a long cold evening in winter, what will you do? Get straight back in the car? Call a friendly plumber? A friend? Stay in and watch the shadows against the wall and soak the silence into tired bones? Go to a bar? How good are you at homemade happy, no other ingredients? Just you?

Do you do 'happy'?

I just want to find something that allows me to shine. Soul ache is the most painful kind.

The story of you is perhaps less well documented than it could be. And that is partly because you don't hold yourself up as a worthy subject for interview. Now why is that? *Because it is just me, not anyone important.* Many of us admit to feeling adrift somewhere between happiness and unhappiness, in the no-man's land between success and failure. Hoping that someone will turn up with the direction, a fast track, summary answers.

You are not alone if you feel the weight of things to do has, like a great pumice stone, filed down those hopes and dreams, maybe even begun to wear away the substance of your soul. Days fly by – and banking on a Tremendous Tuesday full of insight about your future career direction is, frankly, high risk. How many of those have you actually had over the years? Compared with Wearing Wednesdays? Or Shop, Drop Saturdays? Honestly?

What's the big-picture view of your career?

The big questions don't tend to come up in everyday conversation. Where are you going on your next holiday? How is your dad? What are you really looking to achieve in life? Can't see it happening.

Given this dearth of external interest in your precious and wonderful self, no wonder the story of you is still largely unwritten.

But why shouldn't it be a fulsome volume of fabulous adventures? And why shouldn't you start, right now, by asking the right questions.

Strange how we'll ask any number of good questions in our job interview, but fail to ask a single question all the way through school about how to find a career with built-in fulfilment and matching success accessories. Maybe we don't ask the big questions because we don't know where to start. From the thinking and hopefully writing you've done so far, we already have a start. So let's look at what's known about you. There could be info from the following:

- Career highs and lows.

- Fire-and-focus priorities (perhaps worked through with a friend/colleague).

- Your next significant career events, with your ideas on being present when they happen.

It is time to start writing up this story. The idea is that you build up a set of data about yourself that will always help when you come to the next big decision or crossroad. Take ten sheets of blank paper. On the front page, in big letters, write 'My Story So Far'.

Page one: name, age, job.

One-liner from fire and focus: I want to set the world on fire by doing the following:

In order to start doing that, my most pressing practical need is: advice, information, money, time and space – write them all down

Now looking at your career timeline: One career high for me has been:

It was a high because:

One career low for me happened when:

That was a low because:

With that in mind, my big hope for the next year is to start to manage the transition. Eventually I want to be:

soultrader

momentum

That's the start. And as you probably know, starting is halfway through. Take good care of this info – the file marked Soultrader Development is precious.

You are successfully managing the transition between where you are now to somewhere where you will be even more happy, fulfilled and successful. Would it help to cover some of the key steps in managing the transition? OK.

Let's start with some indicators from our web research.

momentum web survey

How do you decide to change job?	Percentage of those who answered	1 = most common response
When I'm bored of the current one	7%	2
When someone offers me something new	7%	2
When I don't feel it is possible to grow in the current one	**85%**	**1**
When they tell me my desk is being used by someone else, forever	0%	3

If I suggested life could improve simply by recognizing your life in a process of improvement, with clearly visible stages, what would your reaction be? Your perspective is critical to achieving sustainable career success.

Key steps:

◆ Believe 'this is transition'.

◆ Work the overlap.

◆ Let go of where you are now.

◆ Arrive.

◆ Get settled some place better.

◆ Believe this is transition.

Getting from where you are to where you want to be

This is about making your next career transition as painless as possible. It's for you if you belong to any of the following categories:

♦ I want to move but I am not sure where or how.

♦ I want to stay and improve things where I am, but I am not sure how or when.

♦ I want to make a decision about whether to stay or go.

> **I know I want to work doing something I believe in and that inspires me, and to work with people whom I feel are on the same wavelength. It's not always clear how I'm going to do this and sometimes I feel I am achieving it; sometimes not.**
>
> Rachel Russell, assistant editor, business publishing

As we saw earlier, you only have to make one of two big career decisions at any time. Get clear on that first. Should I stay or should I go?

The big decision divides into one of two branches:

1 I am going to stay. Is that:
   ♦ Stay and negotiate myself some greater happiness right here. Or
   ♦ Stay because happiness lives outside my career for now. So this job is cool.

2 I am going to go. Is that:
   ♦ Go and do something splendidly different. Or
   ♦ Go and do something magnificently similar.

What did you decide?

'I have decided I am definitely going for one or two.'

Ah.

Maybe a decision-making process would help?

There is likely to be a distance between where you are now and where you want to be. In the middle is the unknown territory, which for now we'll call the overlap. It is after here and before there. The overlap is the darkness we'd rather not get into, simply because it is after here and before there. Even though you might not feel it, I would just like to say that this is a navigable darkness. Which, like other parts of your life, is about to lose it's mystery by being bathed in the light of your soul.

Here are the stages. Unusually, there are seven.

Stage 1 Believe this is transition

Accept and believe truly madly deeply that your career is in transition (even if you don't know where). Allow yourself to feel that right chances are going to come up, that you are on the right path. Might you be telling yourself this is all there is, all you deserve? If you accepted the soultrader concepts, remember you are gorgeous. If you are here, you have a purpose. To be happy, successful and fulfilled.

Do you feel able to move? Or do you think this job is the only option? What would a good mate say to you if you said that?

Stage 2 Face the right way

I know this sounds daft, but you'd be surprised how many people are working flat out on their MBAs and climbing the greasy ladder, meanwhile telling their coach that they want to leave retail management to grow organic potatoes.

If you decide no career decisions for the next six months, and 'just see how it goes', what will you be doing one year from now? Are you facing the right way?

Get some sort of fix on where you want to go (use fire and focus. Now you will start to feel the distance between what you do now and what you'll do in future. Can you see the shape of the overlap? How big is it? Six months? Two exams? A move to Somerset? Keep testing. 'I couldn't do a job with less pay, even if I loved it: what would my mates say?' If your perspective is restricted by fear of approval rather than reason, your horizon will stay just that. Career on horizontal.

The moment we begin to fear the opinions of others and hesitate to tell the truth that is in us, and from motives of policy are silent when we should speak, the divine floods of light and life no longer flow into our souls.

Elizabeth Cady Stanton, 1890

If you desperately love music and want to work in the music business, phone up the record shop, the music mags, the TV stations, the DJs. What could you do to get in and learn if that's what you really want? (Yes, you are hopelessly over-/underqualified. Get over it.) People want to help, but can't while you suffer in silence.

Stage 3 State your wish

Children love stories involving three wishes. What would you ask the genie to grant? A qualification, a chance to bring your skills to the charity sector, or to negotiate claims with underwriters, or to sit with the giraffes at London Zoo? Whatever you want to do becomes possible when you find it possible to think about.

You are more likely to create the perfect job than find it in the paper.

Quenching your soul's thirst, career-wise, requires a little motion on your part. And boldness. How do you feel about that?

Talk to people, research the option, offer to help as a volunteer, ask for help. Go try it – self-esteem grows from action. People want to help – so action is no scarier than telling people you want to find more information.

Do you know anyone who needs an expert on tropical butterflies? I might not now, but if I care about you, I will let you know as soon as I do. When you decide to take action, all sorts of good things start to happen – it is as if a brake has been taken off your progress.

Who could you talk to? When do you think you could have that conversation?

Stage 4 Leap over

This is the most exciting/hardest bit depending on the kind of person you are. The time just before you leave and before you arrive when nothing feels right. You might have stayed because of loyalty to a nice person who brought you in. You might feel your team wouldn't be able to cope. Your might feel disloyal, frightened, borderline queasy! If you are moving towards something that is your soul level purpose, those natural feelings will be in the context of 'Yes, but they want me to be happy'. When people care about you, they want to see you set free on your own exciting journey. When you care about yourself, you want to, rather than stay and complain yourself into an early grave.

Also, remember that your soul is particularly keen to help. You can apply the wisdom of your own four career roots.

Questions might be:

◆ What is my experience telling me about this transition?

◆ What have I learned about myself, about what happens when I am in transition? What/who can I trust and lean on?

◆ What am I passionate about in my new life?

If you are taking steps toward your life purpose, allow your envisioned future to act like a magnet. Imagine the things you'll enjoy most in six months' time and be open to the reality just waiting to happen.

A couple of years ago I worked in a small consulting firm, advising firms on how to manage change. After a couple of years I wanted to leave but was scared of life outside the monthly cheque. Leaving was only bearable because I really could see and almost taste and smell a new life. Fear of loss of salary was paralyzing, so I carried on consulting even though I really wanted to write and work on child poverty issues. The turning point came when I worked out how much I needed to live on (realistic, not punishment, level) and what I could do to earn that. I have not regretted the decision to leave for one second – but it took me a whole year to make it.

Do you feel that you can't afford to leave? That way lies wage slavery – not a term I use lightly. Given the global hunt for talent, and your options to freelance, join a smaller firm, start up on your own – maybe your job is your most expensive option?

Stage 5 Land

'Giant steps are what you take walking round your new firm.'

You have successfully navigated the overlap and here you are, looking back at where you used to be, right over there. What happens when you land? You get the high of newness, new people, new address, new shoes probably. And your huge talents drawn on by a whole new audience. Bliss? Well a high, certainly, almost certainly followed by the dull thud of impact when you land and realize this is good, better definitely, but not perfect. So everyone has a post-new-job downer (well, everyone I know) and that is fine. You are still closer to your purpose than where you were.

Stage 6 Re-root yourself

The putting down of new roots. A time of growth and learning and a few surprises. You realize the ground is a bit more fertile and start to stretch out, grow more knowledge, skills, attitudes and behaviours. Some fruit this year – why not? The new role allows you to feel more like yourself – and in that changing view you decide that something new, eventually, will be a good idea.

Stage 7 This is transition

There are seasons in this journey. Every job has a spring, summer, autumn, winter – every priority might have its own lifecycle. This is a process, a long, easy, enjoyable journey with a great deal of pleasure at each stage. So ... Let's go round again – this time from a better starting place. Decide this is transition. Manage the transition. Arrive some place better.

This is by no means a comprehensive plan – it is a structure to help you navigate the overlap between where you are now and where you want to be. Perhaps re-read the steps and make notes about what is happening in your life, right now.

This might be a good time to revisit Claire, who is getting over her post-not-getting-the-promotion blues.

Claire has decided to leave the bank, to consider working for a smaller financial services company and train as a personal financial adviser. She simply wants to get away from a corporate ladder – which she feels is 'incredibly unfair'. But she isn't sure how to make it happen.

This is where you become Life's Unfair Claire's new best friend (even if you don't care about Claire). It is a chance to use the seven-overlap process. Yes, it seems unfair when you need the advice for your own life. Just work with me on this!

Seven-step overlap process

	Your advice for Claire at this stage	The best outcome
1 Believe this is transition		
2 Face the right way		
3 Take action		
4 Leap over		
5 Land		
6 Re-root yourself		
7 This is transition		

OK. Next is a chance to consider the meaning of life. Oh yeah.

Warning: big life question ahead…

Where do you think your life's purpose springs from?

Where	Answer: yes, no or maybe
Football	
My soul	
The financial goals of the place I work for	
Mum and dad	
Don't care	
God, Jesus, Mohammed, Buddha or another religious source	
University	
My friends	

▶

Where	Answer: yes, no or maybe
Don't know	
Haven't got one	
The kids	
Somewhere in my mind	
Other	

How many yes answers?

Your life purpose isn't exactly an everyday concept, so here is a chance to think about it in practical terms. Consider these questions. Write alongside whatever comes into your mind and then leave it a while. We will come back to it.

1: An angel taps your shoulder and says, 'Hi, I've come to let you know that you'll be joining us next year.' When you recover your power of communication, what do you decide to do between now and next year?

If this was my last year on earth, I would …

2: Your current boss has been told to implement a new staff-appraisal scheme. The scheme is controversial, because it allows everyone in the team to develop their own ideal role, chosen from a list of projects currently under way in the organization. First, the firm wants you to be clear on what you most want to do in life, so they can be sure that your project choice will make you happy. So your boss gives you ten minutes to write answers to the following:

a) I want to change from my current role because of the following:

b) In particular, I am dissatisfied with the following things about my job:

c) Although to be fair, I really like some things about it. The things I like most include:

d) My dissatisfaction might be because this isn't what I really wanted to be when I grew up (and my age doesn't matter on this). I really want to:

e) And when I am doing what I most want to do, the differences will be:

f) Because I am in control of my life, I believe I can start to make changes now. The first, most urgent change is:

Add more on extra paper and attach it to this page. Don't stop if there is more to tell.

So what did that show? That there are some things you want to change? Or nothing? That you want to get closer to the work you feel you were born to do? Or that you can't bear to think about it? Don't worry, this is a filtering process. Allow your thinking to develop, over the time you read this. The key to better outcomes in your career is better questions. So just keep asking those questions – particularly the first one: 'I want to change, because …'

The act of questioning is a kind of self-diagnostic, and like anything the best way to improve is to first of all find out what is going on.

Just saying to yourself, 'My life could be better, and I am the one to make it better' starts a powerful tide inside you.

Who, me? Yes. You're the one who is gorgeous, gifted and unique. You're the soultrader in progress.

PRACTICAL SOUL SEARCHING

What views or subjects make you want to bang your fist on the kitchen table when you've got friends over and the talk gets going?

Can I tell you about Steve, a really nice man who went plastic and eventually became a victim of soul erosion. Unwittingly, of course.

The profile

Steven Marksham (Straitjacket Steve)

Age 42, separated, three children

Client relationship management (CRM) software sales manager

Hope = 'something less stressful, without losing out financially'

Current whiff of life purpose = 'To build kids' confidence as a youth football coach'

The passion of Straitjacket Steve

Steve works for a software firm producing a client relationship management application. He is a manager in charge of five sales executives and works throughout the UK. He works hard and is a high flier at the company – in fact he looks back with only one regret: that he couldn't save his marriage – he has three sons and is separated from his wife. The separation was amicable with no one else involved, apart from, his wife says, his job.

Steve has always had to have the top bonus, best car, and best seat at the annual leadership event dinner. His desire to win and be thought highly of has undoubtedly brought benefits. He can close a sale magnificently and seal off client product concerns with something near to genius. That ability has meant a good salary, good standard of living, and good provision for the family financially.

So what's to tell? Well, the fact is that now Steve has nudged over 40 and has been at the top of the UK sales chart for four years in a row, something is missing. He isn't as juiced as he was about targets, possibly having to act a bit more gung ho than he feels like with colleagues when it comes to the client courtship rituals.

Loyalty to a petrified opinion never broke a chain or freed a human soul.

Mark Twain

Lets leave the client targets behind and think about Steve's soul (his 'vital animating force within'). Somehow, something – not sure what thing – is wrong. And as this might well affect his sales performance, he has agreed to talk through his circumstances. At the risk of you rolling your eyes, I am going to repeat, once again, that soul is easiest to get hold of in the form of purpose. And there are four main ingredients, or roots of purpose:

1 Experience (subdivided into the roots of knowledge, skills and attitude).

2 Learning (subdivided into the roots of risk taking and wonder)

3 Passion (subdivided into the roots of action, choice and change).

4 Trust (subdivided into the roots of calm and patience).

Steve's root:	Questions	Steve's answers
	Steve, what part of your work do you feel most passionate about?	Two things actually. First of all, getting the client really excited about our products, because we will help them get much closer to their customers. That 'aha' moment is great. Second, I love the chance to enjoy the fruits of my labour – I feel pretty passionate about my new car, for example (it's a series-five beamer, by the way; what did you say you drive?).
Passion sub-root: action (defined as the ability to do something, rather than talk about it)	What has caused you to take action in you career? Why?	Although I normally come across as quite an action-oriented person, I am quite conservative in my career outlook. I don't like to make changes unless I absolutely have to – why fix something if it isn't broken? So really, I haven't taken that much action in terms of my career – I have been here for 14 years – long before we started selling CRM!
Passion sub-root: choice (defined as the ability to select the most heartfelt option)	Steve, tell me about the choices you feel exist in your career right now. Is that more or less than you want to have?	Well, I feel this is rather a funny question. I don't actually need a lot of choice, because if you are good enough, the headhunters call you. And I am good enough! Apart from that, I have financial obligations to my wife and our sons, which require a good level of income. This forces my hand – ultimately. Clearly it would be nice to have 100 per cent choice – I'd be on a beach in the Maldives if that were the case!
Passion sub-root: change (defined as capacity to get excited about new situations and create career flexibility to take on new challenges)	Do you feel able to make changes in your life to stay passionate about what you do? How does this manifest itself?	I do, to a certain extent. But one has to be realistic about what can actually be done. For instance, I was a pretty good rugby player in my youth and am tremendously fond of sports coaching. I spend each Saturday with my eldest son's rugby team, helping out at games and generally supporting them. There is a need for the work that I do with that team throughout the whole junior league – and I find the coaching to be really very rewarding. Come to think of it, perhaps even more so now that I have reached the top of my current role. However, it simply isn't OK for a grown man like myself to consider a radical career shift, with my level of responsibilities.

The conversation felt full of unanswered questions – why had Steve become the kind of person who had such rigid ideas about change, about being able to take his career in a new direction. One thing was for sure – he was going to have to push harder at his job to stay at the top, because it certainly wasn't going to come easily. On the other hand, his eyes lit up describing those cold Saturday mornings in the park with the children and their rugby lessons. He became alive and energized, and I could tell that he really put everything into those games.

As a successful sales manager, Steve recognizes and accepts responsibility for his thinking and the impact his thinking has on outcomes. He knows to expect the sale, to work with the client to find win/win results. But somehow he is unable to find the passion to create better results in his own life. It is as if he is bound by some manly code that insists on a stiff upper lip throughout times of soul erosion. So what does the root of purpose called passion see ahead for Steve? It sees a time of frustration and possibly a decline in his happiness and success as he stays locked in his stressful job, with another more fulfilling career within vision, but out of reach according to his current mindset.

What would your advice be to Steve? Do you think he has created a straitjacket with his thinking or do you think he is right?

And, if we can return to your life once again, what would the root of passion see ahead for you? Not an easy question to answer in that format – try going through each of these questions. Bit by bit, slowly.

The root of passion is really powerful because you start seeing what you want. You have to know what turns you on before you can go after it – and yes, this applies to more than romance. What does this exercise tell you about your wants, your needs, your desires? Figure this out and describe it to yourself accurately and you will save yourself huge amounts of time and effort heading off on the wrong career track.

Often people attempt to live their lives backwards: they try to have more things, or more money, in order to do more of what they want so that they will be happier. The way it actually works is the reverse. You must first be who you really are, then do what you need to do, in order to have what you want.

Margaret Young, US author

If you love sports coaching more than software sales, no amount of fittings on a new BMW will make your soul feel good and healthy. If you want to be with your children and pass on great footie tips, no amount of board-level acclaim can bring back those lost hours. Steve, are you listening? Each day away from your passion depletes your soul. Each trade is important – can you learn from Steve's story and give yourself the chance to be more of a soultrader?

How to draw life on one page

Can I ask you another personal question? Who are you, deep down, where no one is looking? How can you tell?

One way to consider who and where you are in your life is to consider what has gone before. But again, you ask, how and where do I start? To find out more about you, we need data.

I trained as a corporate coach, helping business leaders figure out how to improve their lives, based on their true priorities. The company paid a lot of money for these people to spend a day or so evaluating their priorities, not necessarily to benefit immediate tasks, but so the people would feel their employer had their best interests at heart.

One of the most powerful tools I used in those discussions was a career highs and lows exercise, because it creates a summary picture of a career so far. On a piece of paper, draw a line. Start on the left, which can be any point in your working life, for example when you left school or university, or your first job. The line finishes at where you are today. Starting from the left, write down the big events in your career: a new job, a promotion. Show how high it ranked as a high – using your own values. Was the second job a bigger high than getting your qualifications? Show that. Mark each event as a dot.

Also write down the big lows. Write the year next to each one.

The line represents a neutral time in your life. If it helps, write zero on the line and write each high or low to scale. So if a great new job felt like a ten-out-of-ten experience, show it as at the top of the grid. Now join the dots. You should have some kind of undulation – there is no right or wrong here. Simply a subjective record of what has happened so far.

Here is an example. OK, the highs and lows are a bit simplistic, but you get the idea.

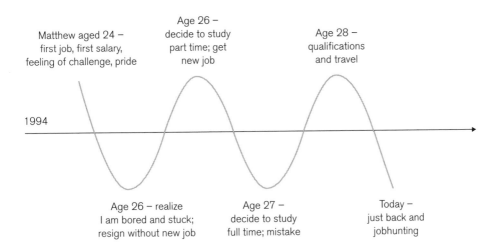

Matthew aged 24 – first job, first salary, feeling of challenge, pride

Age 26 – decide to study part time; get new job

Age 28 – qualifications and travel

1994

Age 26 – realize I am bored and stuck; resign without new job

Age 27 – decide to study full time; mistake

Today – just back and jobhunting

Career highs and lows

Now over to you.

The career highs and lows exercise builds up a picture. Do you see any patterns? What has consistently been the source of your career highs? Legal ones only please.

What about the lows? Do you tend to find yourself out of work or simply out of love with your work? Are there any patterns in those lows?

We tend to repeat the same patterns, whether that is chilli beef noodle on a Friday night or the tri-annual announcement, 'People where I work are unbearable. I'm off.' I had a friend who'd leave his job every two years. He was probably just getting bored, but he had a repeat routine involving his boss turning into a brother of Hannibal Lecter, the (hitherto sweet) team turning into evil fiends. Then he'd go for another two-year stint somewhere else. We could set a clock to his career.

If you find yourself thinking, 'This is what always happens. I could have been a contender, I never had a chance,' or anything similar, hold on right there. Those thoughts are sabotaging your life's purpose – which is (all together now) to be happy, fulfilled and successful.

This is the true joy in life, the being used for a purpose recognised by yourself as a mighty one; the being thoroughly worn out before you are thrown on the scrap heap; there being a force of Nature instead of a feverish selfish little clod of ailments and grievances complaining that the world will not devote itself to making you happy. And also the only real tragedy in life is being used by personally minded men for purposes which you recognise to be base.

George Bernard Shaw, 1856–1950

Fulfilment grows from figuring out your unique purpose, actively choosing work true and close to your soul. You may have thought about this in distant times, when your heart was young and dreams aplenty. But you're older and wiser now, right? Clued up and bordering on cynical. Like everyone else. On good days we acknowledge that work has the capacity to get us up there, feeling full of fulfilment, but mostly we forget to expect happiness, challenge, stimulation. Days go by and the job is just the job, not ourselves joyously riding the wider tides of self expression. Someone else, someone luckier, richer, sexier, is out there having that kind of life, right. But not me.

You know the tasks to be done to bring home the mortgage. You are almost numb with the always-ness of traffic and e-mails and chores. The numbing of your precious self has taken you away from the negotiating table – where there is always a deal to be done on your own behalf. What might it take to bring you back, to present the case for your own success at that table? Are you at the table, or standing near it, watching? If you can bring yourself to sit back down, be actively, passionately in the here and now, you have the chance to make good things happen. You have to negotiate with life to get what you want. The essence of soultrading is to find career and whole-life strategies that are aligned with your highest purpose. How can you find out?

Do you know where your next blast of career sunshine is going to come from – or have you just invested in lots of umbrellas?

The tree grows by branching out in all kinds of directions. None of which have ever had branches before. Those roots take nourishment and sustenance from the soil and transform it into energy the tree can use. What are you taking from the learning in each day to move forward? Each conversation, new job, trip on the train. Every single moment has the power to nourish and sustain, if you use your soul, your roots as a soundboard for your most important questions. Every moment in your life is either an investment in your soul or a withdrawal.

You're searching, Joe, for things that don't exist; I mean beginnings. Ends and beginnings there are no such things. There are only middles.

Robert Frost, 1874–1963

Soultrader goal: finding and honouring my authentic life purpose.

Wouldn't it be nice to know what we were placed on this earth to do? (I sometimes ask, 'What on earth am I doing here?', but that is usually in the neighbour's flowerbed after a top night out.)

Seriously now, please, because this is a very grown up subject. Wouldn't it be great to know where all this hard work and hope is leading to? What kind of outcome is up ahead?

Companies have mission statements, founding values, strategic vision. We have our education, an amount of hope and dreams, interests, hobbies, skills, older and wiser loved ones. Somewhere along the line we devise a believable line on the job we really want to do, and get ourselves employed. It is all a bit random and bumpy and hit and miss. But enough of my neighbour's garden.

Now I am *not* advocating personal mission statements, although there is probably a multimillion consulting niche there. I am simply asking you to stand clear of your daily tasks and resultant brain clutter, to ask yourself 'What do I stand for?' I admit this is a tough question.

You stand for who you are, uniquely. Your mission statement is to achieve your life purpose (yes, I know this may be driving you mad when you still don't know what that is yet). Your values, otherwise known as what is most important to you in life, create the behaviours and attitudes that make up your external face in the world. And it is upon that external face that your life is judged. The tree is one-third below ground, two-thirds above. We don't go out to look at lovely roots in autumn.

If someone asked you right now, 'How would you describe the life purpose of your best friend?', you might know, you might not. Just for a moment consider how your friends would respond to the same question. And write it here.

.... is a person that her/his friends would describe as follows:

She is a .... kind of person.

She/he has the following gifts:

These important life experiences:

These career goals:

Clearly 'what you stand for' is a mixture of the visible behaviours and invisible motivations at the source.

We have never been trained to unpick the ingredients of life purpose, apart from five dull teenage minutes with the 'So what would you like to do, dear?' careers advice lady.

In an earlier book (*Change Activist*, 2001), I said that it is possible to have a job and give a damn, that you and I can take personal responsibility for our jobs and our lives. That simple suggestion, namely to get out there and take action for things we believe in, seemed to strike a chord. Perhaps there are a growing number of us who want to create a better world, as well as succeed in our chosen work and enjoy the material fruits of our labour.

Career outcomes are expected to include greater personal awareness, enlightenment and material success with the hope that those can be achieved without sacrificing personal authenticity. The balance is hard to find, but the fact that we are striving towards that balance is a new phenomenon.

WHAT ADVICE WOULD YOU GIVE TO SOMEONE SEEKING A CAREER WITH BOTH PROFIT AND PRINCIPLES?

Principles are a characteristic of the person not the career. The principles are an input, the profit an output, though I'm not sure there's a causal relationship. You can have principles in almost any situation, but profit is hard to come by. So you can have principles in any career, but if you want profit you have to find a situation with the potential to yield it.

Jeremy, investment banking/securities projects

This is a practical book because being fulfilled by your life and work is a real feeling, as real as indigestion or laughter. You will learn how to track down fulfilment by working back from footprints left by the most expressive part of the soul, your personal values.

By investigating those footprints, we can discover who we are, what we believe to be our life purpose. In order to create a set of options true to your life purpose, you are going to need a strategy, like a project manager needs a plan. Like an explorer needs a map.

By becoming aware of soul level identity, you can plot the right career paths with an accurate compass and go 'do who you are'.

You might want to overcome the taboos surrounding soul-level career success. There are two schools of thought on discovering your true vocation, also known as calling, sometimes sanitized into the phrase 'your career path'. To career out of control is not recognized as a phrase in this context. But it applies to you? OK consider your career from these two perspectives.

Thoughtschool one – the career should be invisible, magic, unsaid and, at the same time, governed by strict rules. You should arrive at your career desk without questions and expect instructions. You will then, once in the first job, play by the hitherto unknown rules with skills and dexterity. Until death, or retirement, or promotion by your local god to enlightnement.

Thoughtschool two – the other says that your career is a process, a flow, and a constant transition towards improvement. One which you will openly question, reassess, define according to the changes going on within you. You arrive at your career desk with your soul intact, acting as a friend who will keep talking to you. And therefore your instructions are a negotiation between the outer world and inner guidance. They merge and balance at the point of action and this is how your life is judged: on the things you do rather than say or dream or forget.

Which of those options sounds best to you?

The idea of your career being a set of rigid activities, unquestionable and somehow not up to you stems from the era of command and control. Like good soldiers, those of us in hierarchical organizations needed to follow orders, meet objectives, and manage for the sake of order and discipline.

Command and control mechanisms worked in organizations like the army, the civil service, where the level of service and customers or buyers of the service were a group with predictable features: 'Tell those chaps in procurement to buy nine million widgets will you, as our customers always like nine million widgets in February. 'Yes sir, I'll go tell the troops.' In a broader sense, the command and control work environment was also a Russian doll within a hierarchical class-ordered society. So we did as our bosses requested (or if you were the boss, what daddy requested) and minded our ps and qs while we did it.

Here in this washing machine cycle of a global information age, a new set of market features drive the fast company. The market is transparent, dynamic and hugely volatile. Companies need flexibility, low costs, intelligence and speed. And as the global market, so the Russian doll of your career path. The closer you are to the market, the more you will be paid in return for personally demonstrating the capacity of your firm to offer the most competitive products and services. Going back to thoughtschool one and the two scenarios, number two was the potential, the as-yet unlived-up-to ideal of the 'dot.com and go' era. It is still do-able. Number one was the job of everyman within companies requiring soul-free employees.

So the context for our career success has changed. Did I say that already? It is because the customers of you and I no longer want the same. The new economy requires faster products and services, which in turn requires a production line that is somewhat faster than besuited soldiers. I believe it needs change activists (a point made in my book of the same name). More than that, it needs change activists who are fuelled at soul level. Change activist soultraders.

People who understand that dynamic change requires action, and that action must be based on purpose and values, not just a knee jerk response. Is that more acceptable?

This change from command and control to washing machine cycle brings both good and bad news. This is useful to bear in mind when asking what career you want to choose.

Good news	Bad news
You have more freedom to choose.	With freedom comes responsibility.
You have more options.	More options, also more competition for the best options.
More chance to think during the day.	More chance to think during the day.
Greater meritocracy, based on supply and demand of market skills.	Reduced job security, and jobs for life now on show in museums.
Greater job mobility, allowing new travel and cultural learning.	Expectation of mobile workforce causes huge economic migration and upheaval.

YOUR TIDE

Have you ever sat on the rocks above a beach specifically to watch the tide turn?

The moment that tide decides to come in, there's something different in the air. You've sat with the gentle comings and goings of water, the current doing nothing special, a soft wash in the background. Now, though, with some internal decision made, it is moving, making a little more noise. Can water be determined? Yes, if you ask the dry pebbles washed over once, then covered maybe forever. Holding the new territories.

Yet nothing else has changed. No big boats around to make waves. The sun still up there, friendly. The rocks, being rocks. Nothing has changed – but look – the sea is now all the way up to here. Collecting surfing bits of wood and seaweed and the odd plastic something, bringing them closer, moving, and obeying magnetism, pulsing onward and further in. Moving as if it has to. It's important.

The moment you tune into your own soul, start moving on the tide of your own life purpose, the same magnetism will take hold. You'll notice a small but charged difference to everything you do. Your tide.

It is waiting to do more than shimmer, wash around, stay in the same place. Your tide wants to come in.

When are you planning to say, 'Yes, I'm ready'?

You are good enough

OK. This is to guide you to the 'vital, animated ' part of you inside, particularly so you can find rich and right answers to the question 'What am I going to do with my life?' Finding your purpose isn't going to happen until you get past the fear of trying new stuff. The normal thing is to fear. Particularly if you have been anaesthetized by large-company life, where the survival strategy of choice is not too much, too loud, ever.

Everyone fears the new. It is fear born from hours of negative conditioning, and it acts like a brake on our dreams. Closing the door in our heads long before day one somewhere new. One bit of research suggests by the time we get to working age, the average adult has mentally stored 34,000 parental hours of 'Don't do that, be careful, slow down, don't touch, be still, quiet please, wash your face again...' All well meant – but in need of an update for the time when you need to put your best foot forward with a firm hand. So this chapter is about coming out as a brave person. Specifically, what you can do to overcome being too scared to try.

Well, first of all, fear is a constant companion through any kind of change. If you are not scared, you are probably not growing. Therefore the ability to deal with fear, especially fear of failure, is absolutely essential if you want the world to hum your tune, salute your sculpture, etc. And you mentioned that you still do.

Fearful feelings might come when you ask, 'Is there a way to try out a new career without screwing up what I do now?' 'Is it possible to shop around for fulfilment vendors, aka stimulating careers?' It is when you are powered by purpose. Buddhist teaching says that anxiety can be overcome by sincere motivation. Why are you looking for something new? Is it to poke your current boss in the eye? To show off a new car to the neighbours? Or to live life using your talents to the full? Sincere motivation is keen to help your life's purpose – and can create urgency. Why wait another year to make your first record when the music is burning in your mind today? It can create the determination that leads to action. Fear is only a spell, broken by action. But you can't do it by thought alone – the new direction needs you to make an effort. Or just ignore it, and run the risk that your fear is keeping you in an altogether unsuitable role.

I know I've got a degree. Why does that mean I have to spend my life with intellectuals? I've got a life-saving certificate but I don't spend my evenings diving for a rubber brick with my pyjamas on.

Victoria Wood, comedian

Purpose is robust. Work with purpose and you can't break your career. It is infinitely flexible. So you can try stuff. Work with status only and the demotion is a killer. Work with passion, trust learning and using your experience and well – today banker, tomorrow sports coach; today sports coach, tomorrow animator; today animator, tomorrow financial wheeler-dealer. As you wish.

There are two kinds of fear. First, stark outright fear – as in you can't use the mobile because you shake so badly. The kind that means your new address is The Bathroom. When it is that bad, there are some major strategies you need to get back on track – ranging from getting some good counselling (always a good idea in hard times) to finding a yoga class. One really useful idea is to keep telling yourself, 'There is nothing to fear' (for more ear-busting strategies, read *Feel the Fear* and *Do It Anyway* by Dr Susan Jeffers). Our literal subconscious just says OK, and reduces the adrenaline, encourages deep breathing so oxygen returns to your brain and you can think calmly and clearly about the seven bull elephants running straight at you.

The second kind of fear is more prevalent. Slow-you-down fear is always just below the surface. Emerging in your career in other forms, such as lethargy, diversions, forgetfulness, continuous consumption. You might just be wondering why you are so tired right now – chances are there is something you are not dealing with in life. Before you get going on iron tablets, look in the mirror one evening and ask yourself, 'What am really I scared of?'

And read *Feel The Fear* and *Do It Anyway*.

On the subject of slow-you-down fear, I'd like you to meet Emma.

Emma's Escape

Emma McDonald (the star of Emma's Escape)

Age 25, married, two children, housewife

Hope = To study marketing

Current whiff of life purpose = 'To write adverts'

Emma's Escape

Emma is 27. She has got two young children, Robert and Samantha aged six and three. Her husband John works for the local council in the works department, so they don't have loads of money.

Emma started a business studies course before getting pregnant with Jack, with the idea of going back to work as soon as the children got a little older. Her dream would be to qualify in marketing, and get a job working as a junior in an ad agency. Day to day, though, that dream seems to move further and further away. In her own words, 'I really enjoyed college, and John was well up for the childcare and everything, but I was a different person back then. More confident – and definitely more slim [laughs].

'Anyway, I was hoping to get Sam my daughter into a playgroup next month, but the deadline for applications was last week and it isn't happening. The day just whizzes by. Anyway, maybe I'll think about it for next September, but I'm probably too old to think about classes again at my age.'

Emma's situation is not uncommon. The slow-you-down fear emerges in the form of putting off the nursery forms, keeping one big barrier in place. The barrier means that Emma can give herself a reasonably convincing story as to why she can't do what she wants. One of the soultrader key concepts is this: Your career is in transition in each moment, towards or away from being happy, fulfilled and successful. Each day a soul deposit or withdrawal.

If you bring forth what is inside you, what you bring forth will save you. If you don't bring forth what is inside you, what you don't bring forth will destroy you.

The Gospel of St Thomas

Emma can find her way back to college – she just needs to overcome her fear. Lets start by evaluating Emma's situation with the final root of purpose. Just to remind you, there are four main ingredients of this sense of purpose and the soultrader tree grows supported by four main roots. Those four roots again are:

1   Experience (subdivided into the roots of knowledge, skills and attitude).

2   Learning (subdivided into the roots of risk taking and wonder).

3   Passion (subdivided into the roots of action, choice and change).

4   Trust (subdivided into the roots of expectation and patience).

We meet at Emma's flat one Tuesday lunchtime to talk through the fourth root, trust. What will this ingredient of purpose be able to show?

Emma's root: trust	Questions	Emma's answers
	Emma, what is working well in your life right now?	Well, we're lucky to have our nice home, John's job is going well and we have our kids. Things are OK really, apart from the fact that I feel time is passing me by. Does that sound odd?
Trust sub-root: expectation	I understand you want to go back to college. What are you expecting that to be like?	Well, like I said to you earlier, I might not be able to – I stupidly missed the application time for Sam's playgroup. So there isn't much point wondering what it would be like. It would have been quite exciting I should think!
Trust sub-root: patience	What if you could go in six months' time – might that be possible?	Not at the local one up the road – but there is one about an hour away and they allow kids in at Easter as well. I could try then – only I'm not sure I could pick Sam up and go to college – I might.
Trust sub-root: confidence	What are you hoping to do if you get on well at college?	Well – this sounds silly but I have always been fascinated by the adverts – the way that companies get people like you and me to buy all sorts of things. If I do go back, I want to learn all about marketing and sales and then try to get a job in one of the advertising agencies – if they'll have me that is!

Emma's fear of going back to college can be overcome by her trust in the rightness of her future role. Her confidence, when we started to talk about various ad campaigns, was amazing. She could remember the detail of washing powder packets, new drink can colours. It was as if her trust in the future had to be expressed before it could work as a magnet to take her out of the day-to-day paralysis of fear.

In my experience as both a social activist and a business person, the cancelling out of fear by trust is one of the most common miracles.

Now I realize that those kinds of sentences can get you looking around in case someone might be looking! Employing your soul as a compass means reading the indicators – trust is one of those. Emma's life is going to turn around, forever, if her trust in the future can carry her past these day-to-day fears of being not good enough. She is, and you are. Let's use those same questions to help you open out some of your own answers on to a wider canvas.

What does the root of trust tell me?

My root: trust	Questions	My answers
	Can you tell me what is working well in your life right now?	
Trust sub-root: expectation	What are you expecting the next six months to hold?	
Trust sub-root: Patience	What other options do you have – is there something you want to do more that might need some planning and care?	
	Might that be possible?	
Trust sub-root: confidence	What are you hoping to do if you get on well with those ambitions?	

Fear creates a workplace lined with potentially difficult situations. And leads to careers that are permanently semi-grown and a hardcore boss you have to face alone. The world is full of friends or full of enemies depending on nothing more difficult than changing your thoughts.

Fear of trying causes paralysis. Trying causes only trembling and sweating.

Mason Cooley (US writer)

However, fear is mostly mirage.

You imagine the reactions of others according to how you feel about yourself.

Did you know matter transforms under the microscope in accordance with the expectation of the scientist?

You are the author of the scary story. Do you remember the event last year? Everyone in the room looked at you when you walked in and decided you barely deserve to live because your outfit is sooooo last season. **So, you can be the author of the success story.** Well, is it possible that everyone looked and thought, 'Oh good, Siobhan is here, must talk to her later'?

You are the author of the scary story. Do you remember last Christmas when you got really ill, probably because you were run down, because you didn't sleep for three weeks. You just couldn't face going back to the office once they knew you wanted to leave to work for the competition. You saw all your colleagues standing on their desks throwing paper clips at you. Horrible. **So, you can be the author of the success story.** Then you got the job and regretted getting yourself in such a state about it all. And Christmas viewed from under the duvet isn't that cool, really.

You are the author of the scary story. Wasn't it awful when no one looked up when you walked into your first school staff meeting.

Then they made you feel so small when you (reasonably) raised the problem with the ladies' loo. **So, you can be the author of the success story.** Is it possible that everyone was just reading the agenda that was given out seconds before you walked in?

Very simply, all you have to do is think away the thoughts you want to destroy, by replacing them with constructive thoughts. This is the key to heaven; it is in your hands.

Paramahansa Yogananda, *Where there is light*

A first consideration, then, while trying for the work, job or life that you most want is to consider your own ability to write the script.

Believe other people care about you and want to help.
You are not a failure for telling others how they can help you. You are a success for opening up to deeper friendship and giving others the chance to do something for you (for a change).

But you can't possibly tell them how you really feel, right?

Fear has it's own momentum, which means that if you cannot bear to attempt task one, tasks two through 200 will become mini-monsters in your head. We all have mini-monster thoughts, for example the task undone coming to grab your precious five minutes' thinking time while you have a shower. The voice that very calmly says, 'You look like something the cat dragged in' moments before you put your good self in front of the interview panel.

The thoughts go like this:

◆ I better not work out what I really want to do, because I might not be good enough to do it and that would devastate me. Better I stay here where I know I can do reasonably well.

◆ If I were to really go after what I most want to do, and fail, then that's it. I'll definitely be a failure then. And what's more, everyone will know it.

◆ What is the point in trying? Everyone knows people like me don't get great jobs like that.

◆ How come I am too fat/too thin/too bright/too stupid/too blond/too dark? for this job. It is just not fair.

Our deepest fear is not that we are inadequate. Our deepest fear is that we are powerful beyond measure. It is our light, not our darkness that most frightens us.

Nelson Mandela (adapted from Marianne Williamson, used at his 1994 inaugural address)

Fear-based thoughts are the reason for so many self-sabotaging career events.

Work is sometimes shorthand for personal identity. For example, how many times have you told people what you do, with the application of just a teeny weeny bit of spin? It is because our job title is the idiot's guide to who we are. And that bothers us. Fulfilment can, of course, be found through challenging stimulating work, but it isn't the only route.

Three years ago I was working as leadership coach to a group of investment bank traders. One of them had recently left, because he always said he would by the time he had a million, cash, in the current account. Aged 28, million made, he kept his word to himself and was out of there. Big drinks, bye bye London, hello Caribbean. Age 29 he was back at his desk, because outside of trading he couldn't find a thing to make him feel as good about himself. Now you could argue, but I think that was just sad. If you move from parents to university to job to promotion to million dollars, I suppose the first 100 days of your new de-stressed life in the Caribbean are going to feel pretty weird. Especially as I don't suppose any of his trader training had included figure out who you are and why you are on the planet. That would be non-core business.

Just to add some balance, here is a true-life example of how to succeed, with personal authenticity.

DO YOU HAVE A CAREER STRATEGY?
IF YES, WHAT IS IT AND HOW IS IT GOING?

Yes, I have a career strategy. However, the means of achieving my career goals has had to be adapted to suit prevailing business and family circumstances. My goals are to (a) become a company director on several ethical companies and (b) supervise higher university degrees. The first goal satisfies my desire for technical and business challenges, vocational challenge and financial reward. The second goal satisfies my desire for participation, community service and mental challenge. I am a Fellow of the Australian Institute of Company Directors and have been part of several company boards. I teach on three masters degrees at the University of South Australia and Sydney University. In these respects, I am on the way to achieving my career goals. However, I found that I spent too much time working and not enough time with my young family. I therefore had to evaluate my priorities and associated timeframes to slow my career a little and devote more time to the things and people who really matter.

Dr Steve Whittle, managing director, BusTech Solutions IT Management Consultancy

My souljourney: freezer girl defrosts

In 1972 my mother, a big strong beautiful Irish woman, died because of a medical error. Aged 39. I was 30 years younger. My younger sister had meningitis as a baby and wasn't in great form when my mum died. She was nearly seven. And so I tried to be mum from then onwards. We had a wonderful dad who kept the world at bay and gave us an amazingly loving home. But my mum was suddenly gone for no reason that my nine-year-old brain could grasp, and I had to find some way to cope. My coping strategy was to put every feeling I had into a deep freeze. Only little things, like my being so accident prone, or so unemotional, would tell people something wasn't totally right. From about ten to age 20, in deep, solid freeze. Age 20 I fell in love and was asked about my mum, and being somewhat thawed at that moment I cried so hard the question was, 'Should we call an ambulance?'

Since then I have carried on defrosting. In fact I have continued the process to the point where I feel warmed by huge amounts of love and hardly any frost at all. This defrosting has consequences. For example, I'm in a supermarket and see someone who is old and with very few things in their shopping basket. I get overcome and want to find a way to help. If I pass a school and hear children playing I want to check inside to find out if every child has enough food and sleep and love and to find out if they have had to put themselves in deep freeze for any reason. And so I am always getting into situations. My sister is the same. She takes people back to their doctors if she feels they haven't been given enough attention.

At this stage I am probably overthawed, because I'm in floods of tears writing this. Which is not in the plan for effective authors for the business market. But this particular souljourney lesson, for me, has been to keep defrosting and risk being seen as overattentive sometimes. Most of the time the love is welcomed. Even if it wasn't, having myself back is worth it.

Do you ever feel deep frozen?

Success: putting it on, or off …

Our lives are built on our habits and the workings of our soul. Now if your soul craves challenge and you ignore it, something bad happens. Maybe not today or tomorrow, but eventually. We are here to express our soul-level identity through everything, including the in-tray.

But is this practical? Surely it is a luxury to cater to the needs of your soul when you have bills to pay, right? Well, yes and no. Let me give you an example. Business wants sustainable profit and thereby builds sustainable profit capacity. The most successful companies over the past 100 years have been firms with explicit, demonstrable soul. A vibrant value system that creates common purpose (for more on these companies, see *Built to Last* by Porris and Collins).

Your career can benefit from that learning. The lesson is that the soul provides depth and resilience. When manifest as a set of values it adds cohesion and consistency to performance. And it feels right. So you can choose an inner fuel source that is infinitely renewable. The power of living as you. Build a production capacity in your own life that you can rely on, whatever the circumstance. Are you able to value yourself enough to tune in to what you most want? Then bear with me while I go on a little soul-detection mission.

Moneymaking can be passionate. Ask your nearest family entrepreneur to tell you about the biggest one-off deal thay ever did. Ask them to stop after an hour! That passion is pretty rare though. We get moments of true aliveness at work, with lots of surrounding dirge and noise. One hundred per cent fulfilment is not possible, it seems. There is some unwritten rule that still requires that we suffer for our income.

What does this mean for our soultrader? Soul doesn't get fed by walking into the office and doing something that inexplicably causes the firm to make a profit. Or does it?

WHAT ROLE DO YOU THINK YOUR SOLE PLAYS IN DAY-TO-DAY LIFE?

Keeps me going, gives me an anchor, gives me perspective.

Karen Drury, partner in Fe3

Few look forward to counting banknotes at the end of the week, but lots look forward to improving the quality of their lives with that income. So there is a potential disconnect between work and fulfilment.

Turning up to do the firm's admin has to be done, the team-development hours put in. Sickies on sunny days stay untaken. You are a good person and you work hard. Hang on. Growing noise of inner gnawing. Isn't there meant to be more? Is it possible that you have become a frightened bright? Listening to a voice in your head that says this job is all right? Best not risk anything, ever. It isn't a brave voice but it is often clever.

The soultrade mission is to skill up on authenticity. Through trial and error, admittedly. One first step is to notice the traffic of thoughts. What is being said? Soultrading free agents have the number plates on each bit of traffic because they put them there.

Apparently our motivation is partially due to what psychologists call career drivers. These are not the same as cabs.

Career drivers are the reason why we do what we do. We become public servants (teachers, police) based on the personal driver of wanting to provide a service. We develop into bowtie-dependent creatives based on the desire to innovate, to be the first to market. This isn't random.

So isn't it logical to suggest that the thing that causes our souls to be fed is one and the same as our inner career driver? 'I am a soul seeking challenge in life, therefore my career is a series of insurmountable challenges that make me happy.' If that is the case, and we can prove it across a range of careers, then fine and dandy: demand and supply of spiritual and financial wellbeing is assured. If it isn't, maybe this is a root cause of today's career crises (which are apparently now 'quarter-life' as well as mid-life; but thankfully, only in America).

So let's check out this theory. Which one was that? The one that says that we are happiest and most fulfilled when we match the needs of our inner soul with our chosen career challenge.

PRACTICAL SOULSEARCHING

What do you do that makes you feel really relaxed and happy inside?

---

chapter three
personal strategies

'Being a soultrader is the best personal strategy for sustainable career success.'

'Why?'

'Because you have a personal career strategy.'

This chapter looks at personal career strategies – what works in the search for a career with profit and principles? This is the chapter that translates what you learnt in Chapter One into your world, your workplace.

You may have heard that eyes are the windows of the soul. In this chapter you are going to learn to use your soul as an operating system. (Yes, like Windows!)

Find purpose, find success – key learning points

Hurrah! You know yourself better. Now you might be wondering how to get consistently better outcomes in your life, to feel sure of improvements that are waiting to flow into your life when you activate this new insight.

Before we go get them, a quick reminder of the soultrader core concepts:

◆ Like it or not, you are gorgeous, gifted and unique.

◆ You have a life purpose.

◆ Your life purpose is to be happy, fulfilled and successful, according to your own definition.

◆ Awakening to purpose significantly increases your chances of success – creating meaningful, inspiring, nutritious work.

◆ Your career is in transition in each moment, towards or away from being happy, fulfilled and successful.

◆ So you'll need a compass. This is your very own soul, there to guide you through each decision, each career trade.

◆ **And by the way, the soultrader is (still) you.**

That 'grow, get, enjoy' activity sits under the banner 'personal strategy'. (And perhaps 'my personal career strategy' is going to sound better in your appraisal meeting than 'my personal fruit-growing strategy'.)

People who are doing what is really right for them (the idea of 'do who you are') are able to give 100 per cent, believe in their task totally and achieve outstanding performance. They can go for it, because the *it* feels totally right. Soultrading provides a solid foundation in an ever-shifting workplace. It helps by defining the intangible something that we know can differentiate in the market – you, your team, your firm and your charity. Doesn't matter. Soultrading, clarity about what you do best and why, gives a confidence advantage, which can turn into a commercial advantage.

Soul is a big, personal idea; life trains us for smaller, impersonal ones. So these thoughts might cause you to come up against constraints born of being raised to engage in trade. We have been trained to consider our self in the concept of a team, a group, an organization. So you may have a strange feeling when you start reading this –

unfamiliarity – because my invitation is just to you. Not you the employee or colleague or consultant or boss. You. The one who has a role but is separate and distinct from that working role. Uncouple them for a while in your mind. This is easier for some than others.

Work world training means that when words like authenticity, personal responsibility and joy arrive on the page with precious little warning, they might not find a local neural network to sit next to. So please allow yourself a momentary pause. Growing your soul level awareness and inner knowing is a gradual process, through which you will very slowly get some quick wins.

The process of finding your life's purpose in itself frees your individuality, and with it the personal strategies that you will need to stand out in a time of economic uncertainty. You untie your hair, shake and suddenly colours can shine. Hair ad moment. You excavate purpose, shake and the fabulousness becomes apparent. Soultrade moment.

More from the momentum website survey

Do you expect to be inspired by your job?	**Yes**	100%
If the answer is yes, do you believe your current work is good for your soul?	**Yes**	44%
	No	56%

From job to career

Is this job my true destiny?

Please circle one answer:

1 **I have a clear idea of where my career is heading**
   Agree/Disagree/Not sure.

2 **I know what I have to do to get to my career goals**
   Agree/Disagree/Not sure.

3 My day-to-day work is aimed at achieving those career goals
Agree/Disagree/Not sure.

4 My career purpose allows time for more than work (e.g. family, sport, travel)
Agree/Disagree/Not sure.

5 I'm known for the fact I'm living true to my authentic self
Agree/Disagree/Not sure.

6 My career goals are financially sound
Agree/Disagree/Not sure.

7 My job feeds my soul as well as my body
Agree/Disagree/Not sure.

If you agree with more than four of those, great. You have decided where you want to go – and you are travelling closer with each day. Less than four? Take a look at the fire-and-focus exercise and start telling your friends to expect some changes …

The hope is that we will find work with capacity to inspire and challenge – more than just any old job for money. But we might not know what that work is, or how to choose it. Most annoying of all, we are not really sure we know ourselves that well. That's why having a personal strategy is really important – to have a way to keep trying to find what it is you want, rather than accept less.

At one extreme of the fulfilment spectrum is the totally unfulfilling job. It feels spiritually tiring, and you know in your heart you have settled for something that will do for now. You are so in your comfort zone it hurts. The day-to-day tasks may be enjoyable enough but that voice of concern, the 'Is this all there is?' question, doesn't go away. The totally unfulfilling job covers you each day like a coarse skin, chafing. But often not enough to take it off.

I base my fashion taste on what doesn't itch.

Gilda Radner

A job that is your highest destiny, on the other hand, feels quite different. Day-to-day work fills you with a sense of purpose, and sustains you. There are simply not enough hours in the day and your work is constantly questioning your talents, asking you to take action outside your comfort zone.

YOUR CURRENT JOB MIGHT WELL BE YOUR DESTINY IF:

◆ You believe people with drive and passion to succeed are cool.

◆ You want to understand how your job relates to others.

◆ Networking in your field is really enjoyable.

◆ If you won the lottery, you would still want to be here and do this.

◆ Friends are friends from work, as well as other areas.

◆ You look forward to getting to work in the morning.

◆ You get things done without worrying too much.

◆ Everyone you know knows what you do.

◆ Your working day flies past.

◆ You want to read anything on how to do it better.

And the third part of this equation is just as important. Fulfilment is not exclusively in the gift of work. You can still be satisfied in a job even when it really isn't the big deal in your life. For example, the many choosers of home over work, perhaps while raising a family, caring for loved ones. Where is the fulfilment in meeting an office task deadline when your daughter has just had an accident at school? Getting thumbs up from the team, while desperately wanting to be with her at the hospital, buying her hot chocolate, waiting for X-ray results?

Humanity requires that the team go do it by themselves for a bit. Say it again, once more with feeling.

The team needs to do it by themselves sometimes.

Soultrading is using that vital animating force within. It brings career success, it also stops you harming yourself on the rocks of duty/ambition/approval seeking, when there are other priorities.

WHAT ADVICE WOULD YOU GIVE TO SOMEONE SEEKING A CAREER WITH BOTH PROFIT AND PRINCIPLES?

Most people define themselves by what they do, and it's certainly a significant thing. But an alternative is to let what you are define what you do. It's hard to change the core of what you are and you're more likely to feel better and do better if you find a career that allows you to do what you are.

Separately, I think people should try and cost things a bit clearer. Careers can be great and give financial and emotional reward, but the demands they make on your time/relationships etc., and opportunity costs they incur through stymieing other activities are great. If you include the value of time spent with your children, of avoiding career stress and frustrating bureaucracy etc., many people might come to a different assessment

John Marchant, co-founder Business360, ClickNwork and Search-On-Line

Personal strategies for beginners

Personal = inner private privy secret intimate

Strategy = method tactics system plan procedure

If you were to look at a day in the life of your organization, the ideal would be each employee happily engaged in tasks that contribute to a higher-level organizational objective. Those objectives would be priorities in the operating plan, itself a key part of the company mission, to achieve its vision. In a nutshell, that is how business is meant to run.

The same is true of personal success, with a personal vision that can be translated into plans, and eventually tasks. Soultraders are focused because the strategy is designed for one overwhelmingly important objective.

To be a human is, precisely, to be responsible.

Antoine de Sain-Exupery

**"Pssst! You should be back at the office!
Vacations are for lazy people!
What have you accomplished today?"**

Steve finds his life purpose

This charts the mental processes taken by Steve, realizing that his job as a software sales executive was taking more out of his life than it was putting in. He wants to become a sports coach.

Perhaps you could carry forward one or two of your ideas about your life purpose – and work through these thoughts as Steve has done.

1 Start

What small step can I take? I need to find a first action that won't frighten the horses. Could I make a phone call? Is there something I could try that I feel reasonably confident about? Deep breath. Start. Start with practical, small, easy. Just pick up the phone.

2 What could I do?

Do I know what I most want to do? Er – what are my interests, talents and values? Have I identified my big destiny? God, what a question! I sometimes get a sense of what my life purpose might be – the coaching job, the kind of people I'd like to work with, the role. The travel, the romance. OK – maybe I dream a little! Now what data can I get my hands on – research, read, talk to people, check out the marketplace, search engines, trade magazines, friends in the pub? When can I start doing my Sherlock-Holmes-finds-purpose bit?

3 Network radar

Could I get in touch with other people like me? Might it be possible to join a project or a campaign or attend an event? Did I keep that website address I saw? What could my friends do to put the word about? Steve is going to make a move. If I become part of something local, surely that will accelerate my confidence – I won't feel like the only one in the world who cares about this. Who can I talk to?

4 Project manage fulfilment

'Self-leadership sounds dull but attached to finding my life purpose, it makes perfect sense. It's even interesting! I have worked out an overall goal, and try to work towards that goal each week. The goal is small, practical, and easy while I'm still getting to know my way round. I have written down what I want to do and why. It gets a little clearer every week – amazing how much stuff is out there once you know where to look. I've bought books, go to seminars, keep reading and stay open and alert! I feel pretty confident that I will stay on track.

5 Fearlessly try stuff

I'm ready to take action – try out those ideas – debate, volunteer, take the job, offer to work part time for free to find out if this could really be my life's purpose. The advice I'm getting from the gang here is don't worry, have fun, experiment. People have got really interesting stories of how they first became involved. So here I am, prepared to negotiate and enjoy the process! I plan to test out assumptions, before giving everything to one option. How is my action capacity today? Not sure. Feeling a bit scared – but I read somewhere that action builds self-esteem – not the other way round.

6 Stay fuelled

How happy do I feel? How am I doing with the work/life balance, good health and generally chilling out? I do feel better these days. I will definitely need to develop skills, knowledge, capacity plus bravery muscle, world vision and ability to eat green vegetables more often to stay properly fuelled. Coffee and cigs might not be the best sustenance for my life's purpose. What else do I need to tell you? Did you know I've started swimming again? And if I want to train on the coaching assistant programme, I'll start jogging again. Oh yes.

7 Keep checking out the basics

It feels easier to stay with the first new idea, so I keep reminding myself to learn more, craft my talents, aim at being better. Do I ask for advice? Yes. I am sensitive to feedback – internal feedback about how all this research and action echoes with my own feeling about my true purpose. I get external feedback from the world – it is saying yes please now. We need someone like you right here. But if it didn't feel right – internally or externally – I'm sure I would feel OK to keep learning, to try other stuff. And at least I would have successfully worked out something I don't want to do. This is too important to get hung up on ego stuff!

8 Refine, define, refine

The local sports jobs don't seem to be landing in my lap right off. Which is a bit frustrating but OK – so I'm busy finding, refining. I am sure that I'm close to home, my life's rightful challenge. It might be salary free, or greater salary. It might clip my wings or allow me to soar. There are no generics – simply meeting my own criteria. Did I tell you I've offered to volunteer with the team on Saturday mornings?

How soon can you start? Is this the week you start to move closer to your true purpose?

Are you souled out?

How healthy is your soul these days?

Not a question most of us get asked. But can you afford to lose it? And how can you avoid selling it unwittingly? What are the early stage symptoms of soulerosion?

Let's take a look at one example – the story of Jake the Jaded. Jake, you may remember, is a whiz at technology-rich corporate events, but is pretty down on himself in terms of his belief that he deserves to be in the role he is in now. Soul erosion – Jake's symptoms.

Soul erosion symptom one: when the core of your job doesn't animate you anymore.

Jake sees work as a way to have a laugh, bosh bosh through the day, then go and get steamed. He lost interest in the technology stuff a while ago. Not sure when. Also, Jake aged 28 is surrounded by bright-eyed 22-year-olds who practically explode with excitement the first time they link two global conference sites via satellite (bless, thinks Jake). They are so up for experiments to make the sound a little sharper, the lights a little brighter, often (for Gawd's sake leave it now, Jason!) cutting into boozer time. Jake the Jaded.

Soul erosion symptom two: faking enthusiasm

He also feels a bit like a fraud in front of clients, which is worrying. He now reckons to be Oscar material in conveying thrilldom when the client says, in hushed tones, that they'd really like Jake and his great guys to work on the next big conference in Hong Kong. Whoop-bloody-whee, thinks Jake, while faking an emotional handshake.

Soul erosion syptom three: growing addictions

At the end of the working day, Jake wants to get straight to the pub, sink two or three beers, and then, when the day has mercifully slid away, play some pool or go to the cinema or out for a major Thai slap-up meal. The pints go on through the evening, and that happens every night. Just to unwind, of course. The funny thing is how many pints get sunk on a Sunday.

Soulerosion happens slowly. Ask yourself:

- What happens if I leave here – am I instantly happier?
- What happens if I stay – can I create a way to be happy again?

Remember the drill:

- Ask questions.
- Get perspective.
- Take action.
- Trust.

- Who can I help today (contribution muscle strengthens your whole career).

- Self-esteem grows from action.

If you sense that something is wrong, it usually is.

You are the only one responsible for how you experience your experience at work.

It is up to you to inspire yourself to make the changes you desire. Yes that might feel hard. The alternative is pretty hard too. Do you want to watch your life unhappen around you?

Ten ways to check your job or destiny

The job is not your destiny when:

1 Your career plan goes through to later this afternoon.

2 The last thing you want to tell your mum about is work.

3 You think friends who rave about what they do at work are total suckers.

4 Life would be great if you just won the lottery. You'd be out of here.

5 You prefer to talk about shopping, films – anything but career stuff.

6 You describe the job starting with, 'It's not so bad' or 'At least I'm ...'

7 It really isn't worth getting to know people because you don't trust them and you are not staying anyway.

8 You don't know the name of your chief executive.

9 Sunday night is written off, pre-mourning the week ahead.

10 Your colleagues don't ask if you are interested in training any more.

If you agree with more than four of these, you need to think deeply about what you are doing, and why.

Careerbot?

This talk of happy days at the old water cooler is all well and good, but how practical is it? In the noughties especially, are well-paid work and self-fulfilment on offer? Well, it seems that even in the deepest recession, some people find their niche and scratch it successfully. Isn't that a horrible expression?

You will find or create fulfilling work if you believe you can. So do you?

You make zero per cent of the shots you don't take.

Michael Jordan, US basketball legend

Lets start here then. Your life is simply the expression of what you think. Soultraders are free in their heads first. Yes, I know this has been mentioned elsewhere. Sorry, but it is really big news!

Would you want to be in your head if the host wasn't home? If instead of you lurked a you-like careerbot? Becoming yourself is the first career objective of the fear-free agent.

Now this takes awareness of your inner being, and an operating system that will allow more people to easily access the benefits. Innerware. Yes, I can see the danger of using IT language to discuss the fragile integrity of each one of us. Lets just see how it goes.

One thing has got to be ruled out if you want soultrading success – making a life within the trappings of someone else you'd rather be. It is phoney and ultimately fatal for the heart and other creative organs. Making a life for yourself requires a compassionate detachment from the identity you portray because you think that is what people want you to be. Careerbot. If you are not fully alive, then you have not accepted the invitation given to everyone who wakes up small and human and confused (on day one and each successive morning). That invitation is to be who you are. To not pretend, evade or ignore this being alive business. To instead increase the pool of people alive on this planet, in this moment, who want to play.

If your work feeds only your body and not your soul, you may as well be putting in diesel. Weasel diesel, at that. Small careerbot portions of mechanized thinking multiply into a career that leaves a metallic taste in your mouth.

There is another way: to be actively engaged in the routinely precious transactions of the head and heart and hand. To disable the idea that you are not able.

Install innerware anywhere

The reality that the ancients were trying to express in the word 'soul' is expressed by defining the soul to be a computer program being run on the human brain'

Professor Stephen Hawking, in *How we believe* by Michael Sherman

What does a computer operating system do? It puts data to use in a way that luddites can understand. Do you remember DOS (disk operating system)? This was an elementary set of programs using text to tell the data stored inside computers what to do.

The next-generation operating system changed from text to pictures and drag-down menus and a whole customized range of word-processing and spreadsheet packages. Although none of my clever colleagues in the big company thought Microsoft's Windows™ would ever catch on because, well, we were sophisticated working on dumb terminals from a UNIX server. Running WordPerfect 4. Does this mean anything to you?

Assuming not, back to the job of the operating system. It is to classify data and make it presentable for a variety of everyday functions. Windows, for example, turns the binary code into a set of easy-to-view screens, which we now accept as being normal PC usage (unless you talk to Mr Steve Jobs at Apple or Torvald Linux). Windows caught on because it helped ordinary PC users do what they needed to do without getting too worried about the technical detail behind it. In the same way as we learned to use our TV sets without getting hung up on wave theory.

An operating system is useful, therefore, because:

◆ It classifies internal data.

◆ It communicates those data in an easy-to-understand format.

◆ It allows a range of functions to be performed with limited technical expertise.

I realize use of the word 'data' is becoming less and less tolerable. Time to make that leap soulward.

As Professor Hawkings pointed out, the soul performs the same functions on our brain as an operating system performs on a computer. It provides the intelligent ordering that allows our lives to run smoothly. The soul creates a set of reasons to go there or not go there, to take the job or not take the job. Some of those reasons are moral, some are more health oriented. But fundamentally, it is useful to know how the soul performs the functions of an operating system. It is my contention that innerware is the best name for this process. Defined as follows:

◆ Innerware is the accessible set of values that we know originates from our soul.

◆ It is the day-to-day measurement of our lives in terms of soul utilization (e.g. as management consultants speak of percentage utilization to describe the percentage of their time that is billable to clients, or computer system management talk about CPUs to describe the degree of system utilization by a set of users).

- It is the resulting alignment of our outer actions with our inner goals.

- You may have heard the saying, 'eyes are the window of the soul'. My suggestion is that you learn to use soul as you currently use windows – to take the inner, hidden information and present it, openly, to the day-to-day world, so you can do what you want to do.

Specifically, innerware:

- Classifies each experience as something to bring you closer to your soul, or as a useful elimination of something you don't want to do.

- Pushes you towards your dreams whispering, 'Trust me – you can do it.'

- Offers a cushion of cashmere encouragement for your gorgeous self, as you try new stuff in pursuit of purpose.

- Reminds you that everyone really wants to help you (as soon as you start asking for something, that is).

- Suggests that some proper food might be good tonight.

- Can display fabulous graphics, stream any movie you ever saw, bring back the memory of the best presentation ever, give you goosebumps on your goosebumps replaying the song you fell in love to. Innerware builds a wave of joy for you to employ, maybe today here and now. And the source is infinite.

- Gets you to turn off the telly after 1am.

- Reassures on the days you don't feel happy, fulfilled and successful.

The only bit that innerware can't do is get you to turn it on. That's what you can choose to do right now.

I choose to use the innerware of my soul to organize a career with more fulfilment.

Inner, outer success

There are two parts to the story of your success:

1 External personal career strategies.

2 Internal strategies.

External covers the part you show the world – your experience, expertise, excellent teeth. Internal is the enabler for external. Every success story has a back- and front-office function, an enabler and a delivery mechanism. Both are interdependent. The individual or organization without soul cannot sustain a public image of goodness and authenticity. As shown in this tale of the BBC.

BBC's pursuit of ratings 'risks the soul of British TV'

The BBC is putting the very soul of British TV at risk with its slide into commercialism in the battle for ratings, ITV's top programme executive said last night. David Liddiment, the ITV programme director, accused the BBC of axing or sidelining fine programmes and serving up an endless diet of medical soaps. The ITV executive appealed for the encouragement of greater creativity, including opening up BBC production more to outside competition and allowing independent producers to keep more of the rights to their programmes.

Raymond Snoddy, Media Editor, *The Times*, 25 August 2001

Personal reputation management

If they were to build a Disneyesque Olde Worlde Management Themepark, we could pay to watch men in neat grey suits taking orders, obeying unthinkingly, displaying zero facial hair and not giving a fig about personal reputation management. We could eat hot dogs and ride through the corridors of middle-range executives in meetings. Flocks of grazing juniors would scurry on the horizon. Tyrannosaurus Boss would thump through a regular find-and-destroy mission. Oops! Mixing my theme parks … or am I?

Personal reputation management didn't matter when we were (a) always grouped as teams or called human resources or intangible assets and (b) less aware of the premium paid for personal attributes in the always-ness of market conditions. At the celebrity end of personal brand value, people buy Tom Peters, Anita Roddick or Richard Branson because they are reliable, consistent message bearers. Tom shakes up the corporates, Anita energizes on social activism, Richard on virginity. Your own brand matters in just the same way: every organization is a marketplace within which you can maximize or minimize your personal capital (more on this in *Float You*, Cope and McConnell, Momentum 2001). Your personal capital is defined as the value any marketplace can put on the unique skills and potential of any individual.

Personal reputation management is important now because you don't have the cover of a permanent team, or a parental boss. So you are you, with your know-how, experience and, tell me – are you dependable, trustworthy, a good person? Because to me, the buyer, those are as important as your skillset. Your reputation needs to be loudly, clearly authentic. But how can you build personal sustainability and a soultrader reputation? If premium is always niche, and niche is about personal relationships, how can you afford not to stand out as a soultrader?

Speech is a mirror of the soul: as a man speaks, so is he.

Publilius Syrus, ~100 BC

Your reputation is a function of two things: your experience and your humanity. Perhaps a soultrader CV template might come in handy as a reputation management checklist. In an age of global networking and 24/7 technology, you sit in front of potential customers every moment of your life.

Soultrader CV template

Answer these questions with examples and humour:

What are your most important qualifications?	
What is your most important qualification in terms of personal authenticity?	
How, when and where are you happiest?	
What are your career highlights? Are they natural or tinted?	
What makes you stand out from others (think about service, contribution and care here)?	
What personal characteristics cause you to be a reputable candidate (e.g. your great project skills, sense of humour)?	
What do you believe to be your greatest accomplishment?	
Who was impacted by that – what did it mean to them?	
What is the most inspiring thing that you have ever done?	

Can you quantify those accomplishments in terms of life enhancement as well as figures?	
What, in your view, does the world need now (in addition to love, sweet love)?	
What do you contribute to making the world a better place (i.e. if you were going to save the world, which part would you choose to save first)?	
Why, overall, do you believe your reputation to be overwhelmingly positive?	
Describe the skills of people who would create a perfect team for you to work with.	
Finally, who loves you? Tell us about your network.	

Answering those will set you up to perform in any soundbite situation.

The soultrader CV advantage is being able to describe inspiring events as well as key responsibilities.

You make a powerful connection with your marketplace when you easily talk about happiness and wellbeing, as well as your role in the 83 IT implementations.

Those things matter. Just remember to assemble this truthfully, clearly. Show it to someone who loves you and ask him or her to make some notes. Does this make it easier to go do who you are?

Great. Next some time with your successful future self. Imagine you are the most successful you can be. A top manager perhaps. Do you think there would be some way to differentiate between you and others (i.e. those who hadn't made it to the top)?

For some people, spotting talent and buying it is the stuff of a regular day job – people such as headhunters and top recruiters. According to Vernon Bryce of human capital firm Kinexa, there are three secret questions (not so secret now, Vernon) that he uses to spot greatness.

They are:

1 As a manager, what do you strongly believe in?

2 What gives you greatest satisfaction at work? (Vernon says that if the answer includes putting in IT systems, they should be a systems manager. The answer to qualify for greatness has got to include really enjoying other people growing and stretching themselves.)

3 Tell me about your success.

Source: *Professional Recruiter Magazine*, 6 June 2001

If these are the questions that separate out the very good from the very best, isn't it interesting that technical aspects of work don't figure very highly. Vernon's three questions, in my view, identify aspects of soultrading.

There is no time like right now to practise your chat with Vernon – or Vernon's equivalent. Who knows when that hour with the headhunter is going to come? So, take the information from your soultrader CV and carry on through.

◆ As a .... what do you strongly believe in?

◆ What gives you greatest satisfaction at work?

◆ Tell me about your success.

Soul-sustaining work is fuelled by strong beliefs, the desire to see others grow, and allows an easy retrospective on success. Those questions suggest a confidence grown less from the facts and figures of hitting objectives (although those are certainly a large part), more the confidence of someone who allowed work to be a fully human experience, who turned up at the office fully awake to growth and development.

If your current role is to be hit over the head for numbers, more numbers and then some numbers later, keep the test between greatness and talent in mind. Your instincts about work being more than work are spot on.

Project name: my fulfilment

Full-frontal fulfilment and happiness won't land without negotiation.

Fulfilling work, i.e. work that you want to do for as far as you can see into the future. Work that encourages you to find and live your values and instils pride. The career-high-and-low exercise shows you the moments when you felt able to take on the world. Keeping more highs than lows in your work can happen. You can design it. Fulfilment can be project managed.

This is the wider context for your personal success. If you were given a job description for being human, it would look something like that. With milestones linked to each objective and a great big juicy deliverable every so often.

Your first area of human responsibility is to love and be loved. Could you describe the milestones on that task used to indicate progress? And what are your key deliverables?

Your fulfilment at work is not separate to your fulfilment as a human being. You can be the brightest, sexiest management accountant in the world, but if you are not seeking fulfilment on the basic human scale of things, your career won't do a thing for your happiness. There we are.

"A good résumé should include some history of volunteer work. So we're going to let you work for free the first year."

So work, like everything else in our lives, becomes an exercise in becoming more human, more connected and more alive. Not more mechanical, more separated, more dulled. Now the trick is to build ingredients of human fulfilment into a work context.

Being a soultrader is the best personal strategy for sustainable career success.

Shall I restate the soultrader connection? I will. The vital, animating principle at your core is your soul. Visible soul is the action you take to demonstrate that it exists. Those transactions form everyday life. Business is simply a multiple of all those transactions. Soultrading is therefore the personal strategy for self-fulfilment in every context, including work. Yes, I know I present big gaps as well as big filled-in bits. Debussy said music was the space between the notes. So listen to what else goes on when you reread this paragraph.

Decide you can project manage career fulfilment (tactic 1)

Project management is becoming sexy. That is, sexy for management which is not the same as sexy for actors, or supermodels or athletes. Or authors, of course. Unless you are a business author. Damn.

For management, getting things done is beyond fabulous. Cinema trailer for management: 'Coming soon to a screen near you – sexy subjects of the future featuring global brand excellence in washing powder and starring "the man who knew how to prevent local photocopier jams".' Project management is simply getting known as a structured way to do the job properly. Plan, do, review is how the Tao probably put it. Countless manuals software packages and the odd 2000 pages of project management methodology is our take on plan, do, review. Unless you buy a jolly useful pocket guide such as *Simply Brilliant* (Fergus O'Connell, Prentice Hall, 2001).

If your quest has a beginning (your birth) and an end (your death), then it meets the criteria for project management. So what about project managing your career towards fulfilment. That seems a fair enough objective.

Fearlessly trying stuff – project managing your life for more fulfilment (tactic 2)

◆ What are you on the verge of doing at the moment?

◆ What single thing have you put off for the last week?

◆ What do you want to get out of the way?

Or

- What do you really fancy trying?

- What makes your skin bubble to think about?

- Who would you ring with an idea if you were without fear?

Authenticity – being your own person (tactic 3)

Are you searching for the experience that will scream, 'This is who I really am'? How would that translate into work?

Align drawn – align what you do with who you are – (tactic 4)

Why is alignment a personal strategy for the soultrader? Because wellbeing is made up of the following:

- Harmonizing your outer life with your inner life.

- Weighing up the intellectual, emotional and physical evidence of who you are and coming to a decision about the best possible life.

- Equalizing work/life ambitions with inner peace.

- Being the same person at home as you are at work.

Let me tell you what I learned about alignment in a Cornish cove on a warm July evening.

The cove sits inside a tidal estuary facing the widest point of the Channel and Brittany (eventually). A £12.99 plastic dingy sets out on her maiden voyage, powered by £3.99 wooden oars in the untrained (and cold) hands of me, plus partner in crime Catherine. Catherine knows how to row a boat. I don't. The sea is very, very cold. There is a small beach audience.

OK. Get in. No points for elegance, so gallons of sea join me aboard. Now the good bit. I prepare to row elegantly into the last sunlight of the evening. Instructions from ▶

Catherine: 'Make sure the oars are straight in the water and move them gently at the same time, in the same direction. To turn the boat, row with just one oar, move in the opposite direction by pushing not pulling.'

I move the oars. Splash, tug, spin to face rocks. Drift. Panic. 'Move the oars at the same time.' Try again – bit better. My next sudden lunging movement causes the dinghy to move full circle again and the beach audience become alerted by strange pirouettes in the otherwise calm water. 'Move the oars gently, that's right. Relax, small movements. OK there you go.' Slowly, very gently. Deep breath. Realize that cold little fingers are in vice-like grip around oars. Loosen grip. Relax. Start to get a rhythm. Drop the oar. Oops. Breathe. OK, away from shore, gently. Relax. Moving. Beach audience loses interest. Catherine becomes more distant as I head back. Zigzagging mostly, but moving.

Perhaps a wider lesson to be had? Let me try to work this out.

When the oars moved at the same time, and in the right position, I needed to expend very little energy to travel smoothly. My small circular hand movements, when relaxed, created nice big sweeps in the water. By contrast, when I grabbed the oars tightly and pulled and lunged, the dinghy went in a circle, or stopped. Lots of effort and no direction. The less aligned, the more effort.

I grabbed the oars tightly and pulled on them mightily, presumably hoping great effort would be rewarded with great speed. Instead I span. When I forgot to keep my oars in the water I wasted energy and didn't really move. When one arm worked harder than the other, I span. When I used small, relaxed but fully composed movements it worked like a dream. It even started to feel right and easy, and my progress into the horizon worked without lots of effort. When I relaxed, I started to do things in the right order: cause and effect.

Leaving the Cornish coast and coming back to you here and now, I am not going to suggest that my adventure points to the only key to success. But as personal strategies go, how about:

- Try to understand the physical laws of what you are doing.

- Get the skill or knowledge on how your craft works.

- Work out basic requirements, like making sure your oars are in the water.

- Do these well, consistently and with rhythm.

- Concentrate on helpful action, and try not to get carried away with your idea of what should happen (I rowed mightily with disastrous results).

- This will lead to results and public actions (the dingy moved).

- It will work better if you don't grab; instead, relax and enjoy the experience.

Or the opposite, fail to comprehend the physical laws, put lots of uncoordinated effort in and spin. Causing more panic and more spin.

Alignment: of your inner soul knowledge to your day-to-day choice of action. The soultrader doesn't grip, understands the physical law, takes the gentle action that makes most impact, keeps going, keeps it moving.

Back on the beach, Catherine said you don't need to work so hard when you understand how to do things and remember to take small, regular steps in sync. Soultraders and sailors have some kind of affinity perhaps?

OK. Back here, with the next tactic to help you project manage your career toward fulfilment.

Feedbackmagnet – project managing your life for more fulfilment (tactic 5)

Surely you and I are not too scared to ask for the truth. Ah. There is a Chinese proverb that says the person who is scared to ask for help is scared to learn.

Shameless optimism (tactic 6)

Expect it to work. Expect your strategies to work and plan for life at the top of your achievement range.

Network radar – (tactic 7)

We are all in this alone.

Lily Tomlin, US comedienne

Build a sustainable network by acknowledging and respecting those who work around you. Create goodwill by overdelivering and underpromising, by doing what you will say you are going to do, by remembering the things that are important to people. We all need the nutrition of care, which, exercised with enough people, over time grows into ethical and sustainable networking.

How many people could you have a conversation with beginning 'I need your help. I want to create a career that feels more fulfilling, with more meaning. What do you suggest?'

Whatever the number, it is possible to grow / give of yourself and gradually build honesty and commitment into your current working relationships – the network will grow. It is possible to develop radar to help find the most nourishing career network – as with everything in project management, what gets mentioned gets measured and gets done.

A fuller vigour (tactic 8)

Stamina, perseverance, getting up when you'd rather stay down, and doing things you'd rather pay someone else to do, with lots of care.

Big destiny (tactic 9)

I'm told that some people fill their lives with crap to make up for not being tuned into higher purpose. Jake the Jaded could easily turn into a drunk unless he reconnects with the part of the work he most enjoys.

Do you know people who have become fanatics (football, shopping etc.) to compensate for the big lack in their soul? Clearly I am not suggesting that work is the only source of passionate fervour – not at all. It is just sad when people give up on their work and transfer their energy and intellect into what could be described as a hobby. Do both!

When you project manage fulfilment, prioritize the important ingredients of your life – that way the other aspects of your life play in balance.

PRACTICAL SOULSEARCHING

On the way home from work what do you like to dream about?

Giving it away (tactic 10)

Success that you have to guard fearfully isn't really success. Yes, healthy competition is good. Paranoid paralysis isn't. Who can you share success with? Soultrading success is an easy companion, not a prize about to be stolen.

That ends the tactics – there are enough good books around on project management (like *Project Leadership* by Briner and Geddes, 2000). Just keep in mind the objective 'me being fulfilled, happy and successful' and start down that personal critical path.

What is your personal strategy to differentiate?

Soultraders are on to this alignment business. Because the first, golden personal strategy is to have what is inside you at soul level, aligned with what you are telling the world you want to be. And to have those aligned with what you are actually doing day in, day out. This is very important. Like anything, locating the 'vital animating force' within you is about asking better questions. Here are a few to be going on with.

For many of us, while our talk is of personal change, our day-to-day actions embed further in one career. That is not alignment, it is fragmentation and will make you unhappy. I know because I have a fragment habit I am trying to break. Alignment means your outer actions in line with your innermost hopes and dreams. Soul level alignment. This is becoming more important. The evidence is found in the seemingly unconnected changes to corporate life.

◆ The 'dot.com and go' phenomenon eroded the concept of the magical breakthrough. We are back in pay-your-dues territory, as graduates want to be in blue-chips and consulting firms again. You might get lucky, but don't expect venture capital to jump out and make you an offer. This isn't 1999.

◆ At the same time, annoyingly, there is a loss of paternal culture in organizations, e.g. HR as the old-style custodians of 'resourcing' are less interested in your career development. You are there while you are there, not forever. So yes, please can you give me the business case for your MBA.

◆ The portable portfolio is as painful as it sounds.

◆ The quest to be seen as the squeaky-clean global brand with no skeletons in the supply chain impacts at team and personal level. Your career will have to include triple bottom line, team playing, environmental awareness, project management, understanding diversity. In addition to your original specialism and any dreaded management stuff you have to do. The budget still needs to be updated.

So to keep up with that lot, you are going to need huge, vast, magical amounts of alignment.

A new view of career rewards

82 per cent of UK professionals would consider rejecting a lucrative job offer if the company's values clashed with their own.

Survey conducted in 2000, reported by *People Management*, 19 April 2001

Alignment is the foundation of your personal strategy. If it all goes well, you could expect these kinds of rewards:

- The chance to learn, create, fall on your bottom, and survive in a supportive environment.
- A better sense of self, and lots of quiet confidence.
- Personal brand equity, where integrity translates into high-trust networks.
- A track record of good clean wins – building up an ethical track record.
- People who would buy you tomorrow if the firm went under, and would be happy to poach you now (if it wasn't morally wrong).
- Team-spirit mushrooms (your team are fungi to be with).
- A range of career options, all over the world. Harvested from those high-trust networks (yes, that sounds cynical, but I promise it doesn't have to be).
- Access to capital. Will those allies back you with their dollars?
- Wellbeing. Fit in mind and body and spirit?

Does that sound like a new set of measures for career success? Does to me.

Soultrader measures success differently.

Success has traditionally meant a place high up in the hierarchy, material benefits and the chance to exercise power.

Given the faster global agenda, and the rise of the free agent, is that still the case? Or is income a partial reward mechanism for the soultrader? Perhaps the following are part of the new deal. Consider what you are doing for a living right now. Does your current job enhance your:

- Creative capacity
- Self-esteem
- Network

- ◆ Ethical track record
- ◆ Allies and advocates
- ◆ Opportunity to drink, laugh and love (even if drink means lattes)
- ◆ Global reach
- ◆ Access to capital
- ◆ Health?

What role has soul at work? – a web survey (2001) (**www.yourmomentum.com**)

What do you expect your job to give you?	1st	2nd	3rd	Average	1 = most common response
Security	10%	7%	3%	6.6%	6
A career network	3%	7%	10%	6.6%	6
Learning and growth	**39%**	**45%**	**7%**	**30.3%**	**1**
Self-esteem	3%	7%	14%	8%	5
New skills	0%	14%	21%	11.6%	4
A paycheque	**16%**	**10%**	**28%**	**17.3%**	**3**
Drinking buddies	0%	0%	0%	0%	
Fulfilment as a person	**29%**	**10%**	**17%**	**18.6%**	**2**

Are you doing the work that you've always wanted to do?	Percentage (of those who answered)	1 = most common response
Yes	19%	4
No	26%	2
Don't know what I really want to do	22%	3
Yes – on the way	33%	1

I realize there is a danger here of putting forward a simplistic argument. Doctors would perhaps argue their soultrader status is irrefutable, as they already answer their highest calling. They save lives. My contention is that the doctor who is saving lives and living without any sense of personal need or fulfilment is in danger of losing one life, his or her own, through the daily drain of life on call. Given that the soultrader is someone who:

◆ Understands and employs the vital animating force within to achieve career fulfilment.

◆ Is energized with purpose, on the road to personal fulfilment, wealth and happiness.

Doesn't that definition automatically apply to the people who are deeply engaged in professions with huge amounts of contribution? Surely huge fulfilment is the big personal payoff for life on the hard road of 'a caring profession'?

Well I'm not sure. It might be soultrading or it might just be another surface you've created. Is that possible, nurse? The daily wiping, smiling and caring. Cleaning a patient's face after Thursday's fine hospital breakfast. Dreaming of a cigarette, now please, with the hunger of someone who would swap eternal paradise for five minutes' peace in the car park.

Even in a caring profession role, there is still the same danger of being in an orbit of borrowed to impress. Whizzing round and round. This is what is right and best for me to do and look how well I cope. Now next blood test. Shall I direct my thoughts to more smiling or just absorb some foreground? The soultrader contention is that service with a smile is dysfunctional, most of the time. It could usefully evolve to service with a whatever I happen to be feeling and would rather be honest right now thank you. What is the point of grinding through a career that you originally chose for external approval and hating it?

What is wrong with deciding on a change, choosing to do what you most want to do, because it feels right? Is that possible? Not where I work, I hear you think. Never in a million years. Well if it isn't going to happen where you are now, maybe this book can help you find the place where you *can* express who you are. Which will help you go do who you are. To create a career path and life purpose that merits all your time and energy.

Yes, I realize that means you will have to change and this probably feels more horrible than going on with a heavy heart. It is OK. Once you decide to make a change, things will go right for you, so trust your instincts. Things stay hard when you are not on your right path. This is almost a universal law.

Some questions for you:

◆ When was the last time you felt really animated about your life?

◆ Ditto, re your job?

◆ When were you last held in the tracker beam of a challenge that meant everything to you (evidenced by, for example, the fact that time flies, you have to tell everyone all about it, you felt the outcome was absolutely all engaging)?

◆ When was it?

◆ What were you doing?

◆ Who else was involved?

Let's try another angle.

◆ When was the last time you felt restless, uninspired, lacking a sense of personal direction?

◆ What were you doing?

◆ What was going on?

◆ Hands up if this feeling is familiar.

◆ Do you feel this right now in your life?

- Feet up if you want this to change, if you want to find out what to do when you grow up (equally applicable to over-50s).

- Stand up if you are willing to change right now.

Did you move just then? OK. Do you want to re-read the questions and consider whether or not you might like to move?

I wonder if that is something that we would be able to do if we could think like free agents. Find a way to remake our current jobs with more purpose, start fresh, and tackle everything with more enthusiasm. I wonder if our jobs would become what we really wanted to do all along if we just had the chance to restart them now and again.

Whether you work in a big organization or for yourself, the term 'free agent' may not ring your bell. However, you probably recognize that some time in your career, whenever that is, you will need to speak from your soul to the job market. There is simply no point asking for happiness if you cannot find a way to define your purpose, and go do who you are (aka soultrade).

Do you know of anybody who took a risk in their career to become more truly who they are, and looks back with regret? I don't think I do.

There are many things I do regret though. The time I tried to be a smooth jazz singer. Friends could have told me more forcefully that listening to me on vocals is soothing, in the way the grinding of walnut shells is soothing.

Surface or authentic career

This business is completely about surfaces, so it is important your surface is well maintained.

Actor Tom Hollander, *In Style*, May 2001

Are there genuine smiles all round as you and the team deconstruct your well-constructed brokerage deal? What about those loud hearty discussions with new clients in the hotel bar? Do you wonder how much longer you can feign delight at their improving market share? You drive back in a very nice car not really savouring the oily taste of your post-appraisal dinner with the head of innovation.

Tomorrow brings a whole new pitch. With matching linen outfit.

Lets take a look at your career right now. Chances are it looks good and it is, provided you keep up the payments, all yours. Life in the fast lane requires that you maintain your surfaces. Because sometimes that is all there is. Your career priority is to buff the presentation material. The animation. The colour. The images. Not Powerpoint. This is your surface we are talking about.

Now what gets worrying is when this image is the artist formerly known as you. Why? Because you can't pretend all the time. You need to be you, not used. You are rich and right , your office filled with natural light. And you need every drug to sleep at night. What happens when you strive for great surfaces? You get great surface level success. Which is fine but not all that life has on offer. So why aim shallow? And another thing. There is a surfeit of surfaces. I am not saying every beautiful surface is shallow, but a characterful face wasn't born through immaculate complexion.

Are you ready to take a look at your life?

chapter four
make better career decisions

'Being a soultrader is the best personal strategy for sustainable career success.'

'Why?'

'Because you make better career decisions.'

You can learn to make good career decisions even if you don't know the first move to your life's purpose. Even if all you feel is 'there should be more to life'. Soultrader will help you create a more inspiring, truer career. How? By steering by what is most important to you.

This chapter considers the overall mental adjustments you need to make to be a fully-fledged soultrader. It concentrates on exercises and take-to-work plans to make the transition from where you are to the next level of happiness, fulfilment and success. This is the chapter to check through all your previous intentions into a personal action plan.

Earlier I suggested that you only ever have two decisions to make in your career. One: stay. Two: go. Perhaps broken down into two further categories.

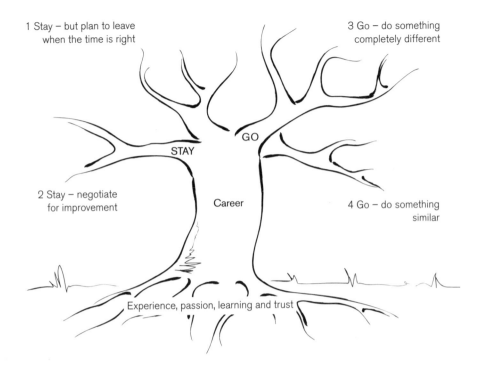

1 Stay – but plan to leave when the time is right

3 Go – do something completely different

GO

STAY

2 Stay – negotiate for improvement

Career

4 Go – do something similar

Experience, passion, learning and trust

1 Stay and do nothing

Mindset = I am in transition, ready to take action when the time is right.

2 Stay and negotiate

Work out what needs to improve in order for you to feel happy, fulfilled and successful. Decide to make improvements and stay.

3 Leave for a new but similar job

Move job and stay in the same field to be closer to what feels like your life purpose.

4 Leave for something completely different

Create something completely different for yourself.

So out of those four decisions, where are you right now? Are you a one, two, three or four? Right now it is fine to be nearly or definitely all of them, as long as you choose at least one.

How can you make a better career decision?

The four have enabled Jake, Claire, Emma and Steve to understand what is going on for them. In addition, the various soultrader tools and techniques have been encouraging them to overcome fears, create a set of strategies, and generally give their dreams a decent airing. Each one of those four decisions can therefore be filtered through the roots of purpose. Like this – please circle the answer most true for you.

My career decision is firstly to go or stay.

- I plan to stay and bide my time and be ready to act.
- I plan to stay and negotiate so I feel happier.
- I plan to go to something similar.
- I plan to go do something different.

(Please note: there is no 'I don't know' category. Time to look your future happiness in the face.)

OK. Write your chosen decision here, with some more detail. Tell me what you plan to do, what it involves.

I plan to:

This next exercise will help you to ask the right questions and check out what might help or hinder your decision.

Career decision health check – experience

My roots: experience	Questions	My answers
	I know what I want to do next – just not sure if it the right decision.	
Experience sub-root: knowledge (defined as information and understanding)	Have I got the right know-how to succeed in this new decision? What else might be needed?	
	Does this direction really interest me? (for example, if I got locked in a big bookshop for 24 hours, would I want to read up on this?)	
	Who can I ask? Can I find someone who has been there, done the transition with a T-shirt to lend me?	
	Am I happy to put in the effort to make this work – really? This might mean research in the evening, taking time off to meet people who could help, reading everything I can get my hands on. Am I motivated enough to do that?	▶

Experience sub-root: skills (defined as the ability to do something)	What kind of skills am I likely to need in this new choice? Are these the skills I most want to use? (Surely I've got enough customer-problem-solving skills now – why can't I try out my presentation skills?)
	What are my transferable skills?
	What skills are going to be needed to make a go of this? Have I got them?
	Who can I ask?
	Am I happy to put in the effort to make this work – really?
Experience sub-root: attitude (defined as temperament or approach)	What attitude will I need to make this new direction a success? Do I need to be passionate, patient, enthusiastic, energetic?
	Who can I ask?
	Am I happy to put in the effort to make this work – really?
A phrase to say to your inner critic to help wash away the mocking words we all hear	This is OK – it's only change. I am in control of my life. I make good career decisions.

You'll notice that two extra questions are being asked at this stage – who can help, and are you prepared to put your back into this to make it happen? Jot down ideas at this stage – don't worry if you can't fill out each box. You've started – that's the main thing. Making a good career decision is simply this. Decide the direction and then keep taking baby steps in the same direction.

But I don't know the direction!

Yes, alright, none of us has a crystal ball. The direction is the next moment following what is important to you. And then the next. Not a five-year plan. Take baby steps – ask someone if they know anything about what interests you. What would they do if they wanted to find out more? Do they know anyone who works there? Do they have a website? Find the overlap between where you are now and where you want to go. The overlap is right there in front of you – it consists of:

◆ Questions you can ask.

◆ Dreams you can dream.

◆ People you can ask.

◆ Information you can access.

◆ Action you can take.

See page 68 for the seven-step overlap process.

You don't need all the answers – just the right perspective to start asking questions. People want to help you. You help people right? Oh – you're a total no-give. Ah. Do you want to sort that out first?

So you have decided that the film industry doesn't juice like it used to (this happens, believe me) and you want work with more social contribution. Now, what questions can you ask – talk to Voluntary Service Overseas (VSO), tell them what you've got to offer. OK, maybe they won't want a full-length feature on life in rural Uganda – but they probably want your project skills, your creativity.

Use the questions above. Dream – see yourself out there on the project. Get the information, take the action.

Purpose is the day-to-day manifestation of your soul. You have a purpose – to be happy, successful and fulfilled. Believe that and use that belief to enquire – keep adding to the store of information about your desired direction and before you know it you will have made a great career decision. Fulfilment is a gradual change, like spring.

Between two evils, I always pick the one I never tried before.

Mae West

Trust this process of asking, defining, refining. It isn't instant but hey – you didn't want to do a megaleap into the unknown anyway.
It works – soultrading is magnetic and life wants you to be happy. All together now – oh no it doesn't, oh yes it does! We could be here for hours. What is your perspective? Decide to be happy.

Now, lest I come over all botanical again, lets look at the next area of investigation for your Great Career Decision. This next exercise looks at the root of your learning. The exercise is aimed at those pre-career decision times – when a soulward career move is needed but elusive. Two of the soultrader concepts might help here. When you feel a bit lost, remember you only have to decide, at high level, to stay or go. Then remember:

◆ Your career is in transition in each moment, towards or away from being happy, fulfilled and successful.

◆ So you'll need a compass. This is your very own soul, there to guide you through each decision, each career trade.

The next exercise is for anyone ready for some career transition – without as yet knowing what.

Career decision health check – the roots of my learning

Roots of learning	Questions that might help	My answers
	I want a career that feels more like my life's purpose. But I don't know what that is.	
Learning sub-root: risk taking	Am I up for something new? Or am I better off staying? How much change is happening in other parts of my life right now?	
	What would I try to do if I knew I couldn't fail?	
	Or – what would I choose to do if I had enough money to make a limitless choice?	
	Who can I talk to – who knows me and might help?	
	Am I happy to put in the thinking time to work this out?	
Learning sub-root: wonder	What do I really enjoy doing – outside work as well as inside?	
	What makes me feel like a child again – excited, or overawed with wonder? Is it the buzz of winning a match, or more the feeling of being	

▶

	part of a community doing something to help others? What juices me?
	When was the last time I felt really excited about something at work? What was going on?
	Who can I ask? Who knows me well enough to tell me what lights my fire at work?
	Am I going to ask them – am I going to invest in the story of me?
A phrase to say to your inner critic to help wash away the mocking words we all hear	My life goal is becoming clearer to me – it is important, inspiring, and I am the one to make it happen.

Soultraders expect happiness.

The consistent message is that when you get clear on who you are, you make better work/life decisions, locate more elegant career solutions, and live as your true self.

How about we translate soultrading theory to you and your place of work? If you want to stay and work on inner wellbeing for a while, an idea for more background reading is *The Art of Happiness* by His Holiness the Dalai Lama, *The Power of Spiritual Intelligence* by Tony Buzan and *Jonathan Livingston Seagull* by Richard Bach.

Is yours an accidental career?

Some careers are almost pre-destined. Marion always liked animals, so she became a vet. Easy. Michael age 12 is mad on computers so he takes the exams that would allow him to become a systems engineer. And play with computers for years. Easy.

Some are less clear. Lara likes TV soaps, hanging out with her friends and Tomb Raider, so she went into insurance. Daniel likes logic problems, circus and gardening so he became a home security alarms adviser. The accidental career is everywhere. How did you come to be doing what you do now? Did you always know you wanted something in this area? Did you end up with your current job for another, fluky reason?

But your accidental career is actually a very cool starting point. In fact, finding your way in an accidental career is not any harder than finding your way in the job you wanted since childhood. There are always the four directions, ways that you can branch out from where you are now.

Every job is a transition point, a place that feels right for a while. Then, as you grow, the job needs to grow with you or you need to move on. Perhaps it is time to accept that our careers are examples of perpetual motion, the market shifts, your expectations shift, the contract shifts. For a brief moment it all seems aligned. Then out come the doubts. Each job has a natural lifecycle, a honeymoon time, a slow time, a 'my boss and I are not getting on' divorce time. If we are perpetually wondering if this is still right, what can help to perpetually check our bearings? The degree of rightness for me personally right now? What might stay aligned even when we are not sure which way our lives are meant to face?

One answer might be to check in with the part of you that remains most concerned with your best interests: your soul (admittedly harder to e-mail). But how?

PRACTICAL SOULSEARCHING

In your own time machine, what date would you visit?

What would you do there?

Why work at all?

Daily life – unless you were born 'independently wealthy' of course – is largely taken up with the repayment of a debt established somewhere before our time. The almost imperceptible norm of acquiring debt for our old age, slightly mitigated by the crumbly base of pension funds and the like. The idiocy of feeling in debt for most of our working lives when we work harder, year on year, than we ever expected to.

Without a financial windfall dropping into the cradle, our standard of living depends on our parents' good fortune and free agency followed by our own wit and wisdom, finally landing right there where you work right now. How much do you get into your account each month? And how much goes straight out again? Almost all? Me too, and I am beggared if I know where it goes. Probably to the parallel universe of single socks. Piles of 20-pound notes and all my poor sport socks, sitting together in the 'lost by Carmel McConnell in transit through life' pile.

Income level defines our day-to-day comforts. You want to live where? How much do you earn? How much can you save? I'm afraid not sir. So sorry. You want to travel to, oh round the world, you thought. Nice dream. Not fair, I know sir. Yes, I know it wasn't easy. Remind me again, sir, of how much you managed to save last year. Two hundred and seventy-four pounds and 14 pence. Well done. Would a long weekend in Robin Hood's Bay be OK? Perhaps sir would like to cry in someone else's arms, sir. Thank you.

Cyberserfs

> **Cyberserf:** *noun*
> employee of the global technology/knowledge economy whose day job will never be enough to create surplus personal wealth

Let's get some historical perspective.

Traditionally we earn in direct relation to what we own.
Land (capital) equals crops equals income. Factories (capital) equals shirts, or other product, equals income. Without land to tend, crops to grow and eat, or the odd factory from daddy, we have inherited a world of tithed employment.

The strange thing is that today we have web pages and 400 cable channels to commentate on everything, but seem to have a collective amnesia on the reasons why we all get up and go to work to pay off our debts.

Like that is normal. The taboo question is why we are in debt and online and how did we wind up cyberserfing? Working with technology to accumulate more personal debt? Working in a global knowledge economy where the gulf between haves and have-nots is widening. Technology tethers the employee to the office. Hours have increased, with a decrease in overall earnings (see *The Ownership Principle* by Jeff Gates has more on this).

It doesn't add up personally, nationally or globally. Let's stay personal please, begs reader. OK. As long as I can quickly mention that society is simply you and I and our pals and the people we work with, multiplied by however many towns and villages exist in our countries. That's all there is, just you and me and more like us. No leaders, no grown-ups. No one with a plan that is being implemented. The great myth of global trade agreements is that there is some overall strategy for universal wellbeing. There isn't. From where I stand, current structures of corporate and national ownership equals access to even more resources and bully-buying power. Not the improvement of ordinary individuals around the world. Yes, I know, countries benefit from international investment. But just look at the data on the corporate watch website, or read the reports by national government organizations (NGOs) such as Actionaid or Red Cross. Global poverty is increasing, at a time when consumerism is more rampant across more global markets. You and I are powerful soultraders, and we can make a difference – starting with some basic economic evaluation of the personal profit-and-loss account.

We work to make a profit for our employer (or our own firm) by applying our specialist skill and knowledge, in a consistent day-to-day effort. This is the core of going to work. More personal profit leads to more personal choices. But day-to-day saving seems hard.

As hard workers we learn how to be even harder spenders. Result = cyberserfdom.

Very few earners can save it faster than spend it. So our treadmill is formed. We have unprecedented levels of consumer debt.
The 'engines of growth' are hard to find. And yes, slowdowns are cyclical.

Buying our lifestyles has resulted in a strange relationship with our career. It has to be lucrative rather than luminous because, well, we're broke!

We want worthwhile, dream of inspiring, but the bottom line is we'll settle for being in credit at the end of the month. I wish it were different – that fulfilment and free agency could be defined and created in a free environment. But let's be real. This is a deal that suits the directors of our global economy. And in these early stages of the knowledge workers return to free career choice, that's fine. We can work with that.

Given this distinction between inheritance and earnings, the first rule is to accept responsibility for your personal situation and define what is happening with the intention of improving it, not bemoaning it.
For starters, what do you earn and how do you earn it? Does that income give you freedom to not go back to work next week if you so choose? Or is the money going out each month about the same as the money coming in? What is the likely outcome if things stay the same, in about ten years' time? I am happy to hear the answer 'good times'. So you feel things are generally positive and improvement is generally possible.

That's great. You are looking forward to good times, yes, and I would suggest you should also be aware that this future comes with certain conditions. Called employer rules. For instance, no leaving the country for three months without permission. No unannounced change of career without financial penalty. No questioning of the basic contract without consequences: 'You are disappointing us. We had high hopes for you. We thought you were happy.' These rules are the conditions of cyberserfdom, and are very comfortable for most of us who are used to the routine. For fulfilled free agents, these conditions chafe unbearably. How do they feel to you?

Waking up to your whole range of potential career choices does risk asking questions that may mean you become 'a troublemaker'. Before you go off looking for www.spartacus.com for ideas, let me offer a few gentle pointers. It is possible to navigate out of any conditions that do not feel absolutely right to you, without risking too much financially. Financial risk isn't sensible right now (what with the new house/baby/kitchen/holiday/teeth). Is it?

Taking control over your life depends on your ability to find and own a form of capital that makes money without relying totally on your daily effort.

Your daily effort is simply a perishable commodity in a global marketplace. Can you get hold of longer-shelf-life commodities such as property, specialist knowledge, or land? There is a journey to be made from cyberserf to free agent. And my question is, from where you are now, do you feel that to be a trip worth making? How will you motivate yourself to try something different – when the existing system is so, well, normal? And persuasive. And being in debt is OK provided the conditions are comfortable.

Quite reasonably you would want to know what is involved in the journey. What has to happen. Well my idea is that this book will be a guide to you inside, to help you assess whether or not you want to make that journey to more sustainable career success and fulfilment. Becoming aware that you want life to be better is the first step; lots of books can tell you that. The question has always been how to keep going once you realize life has to change. Well some of it is about self-definition. If I suggest that you, and you alone, are responsible for your ability to soultrade, you might not like it.

To travel from indentured worker to free agent is to become energized with purpose and clarity.

The best way to understand your destiny is to employ the vital, animating principle inside you as fuel, as motivation for the road.

The best way to make progress on the road to free agenthood and personal fulfilment is to travel as a soultrader.

Now at the risk of repeating myself, I want to restate step one of the journey. Accepting personal responsibility for your career, your life in fact. This breakthrough marks a difference between the real haves and have-nots. And ultimately between those who choose cyberserfdom indefinitely over free agency.

Now I know this personal responsibility nettle is hard to grasp. There is a much more comfortable ride available back there in the car marked 'they won't let me' but it won't go as fast. So try saying these sentences to yourself: 'I am responsible for what happens in my life. I am responsible for my career choices.' Now say them again. Did you hear, 'Oh no I'm not, because I didn't get the education I wanted' or 'Oh no I'm not because I'm not allowed to'? All that stuff is simply background noise, a critical voice from our years of hearing criticism and parental concern. The voice to start turning up is the one that says, 'Go on, you can do it, have a go.'

That's your soultrader speaking.

I would suggest that you are also responsible for the degree of ownership over your career. We choose to own and steer fully, partially or not at all. We can ask to be owned, and steered, by employers. But that way madness lies. This horrible thing called career responsibility is a bit of a fright at first; how can anyone know what they'll want a few years down the line? And isn't it reasonable to hope that someone a bit higher up in the company has some kind of plan, encompassing our small but valuable contribution? Madness lies that way also.

I suppose one of the ways to spot a proper leader is through their awareness and expectation of career ownership. If you were to take a quick mental audit of people you work with, how many know where they want to go, and are creating opportunities off their own back to get there? Go on. What do you think your colleagues would say about you, asked the same question?

Executive pay at the [US] nation's 365 largest companies rose an average 481 per cent from 1990 to 1998 while corporate profits rose 108 per cent.

Had the typical worker's pay risen in tandem with executive pay, the average production worker would now earn $110,000 a year and the minimum wage would be $22.08.

Source: Sharedcapitalism.net

There could be a metaphor here: the difference between owners and workers is like the difference between wealth in the form of capital and wealth in the form of income. Capital makes income. Income is produced from capital, it is a return on the capital investment. Another aspect of the haves and have-nots in terms of personal responsibility is the ability to analyze in terms of income and capital. Those of us who take ownership of our careers are more likely to view our work as an area of capital investment, from which income will be generated. With that perspective, careers are a way to create money, which in turn makes more money. For example, you may clean windows for a living. That set of skills – cleaning, keeping customers happy, doing the accounts – can be distributed via subcontractors. Eventually you may have ten window cleaners working for you and can reasonably expect, eventually, to have no need to go up a ladder again. That is shifting your career from income production, to capital production.

Career-ownership have-nots, on the other hand, have jobs that produce an income. That income is produced by a daily exchange of

labour and skill and is dependent on personal attendance.
For example, you may clean windows for a living. You will expect to
go up a ladder every day for as long as you can. And from that
perspective, you will have little expectation of being free to leave
your job. You are renting out a career, not owning it.

Career ownership versus career rental. Know the difference. Serious money rarely comes from sticking with the day job.

Now the career guide books don't mention this. Strangely. Is being a
non-owner so all-pervasive? I suppose it is. I always think everyone
learned this before me, so I am keen to pass it on There is a way to
get out of surviving at the mercy of market conditions or the boss's
mood. It requires your decision to steer your career.

chapter five
work just changed, forever

'Being a soultrader is the best personal strategy for sustainable career success.'

'Why?'

'Because the world of work just changed.'

Work that is more than work

Work is becoming an expression of our spiritual, as well as material, ambition.

Whoa there. Hang on. Why? For the following reasons:

◆ Standards of living have increased, so according to Maslow's hierarchy of needs, there are more of us at the 'self-actualizing' stage of our lives. We therefore look for our work to offer an opportunity to find self-expression at all levels, including spiritual fulfilment. (American psychologist Abraham Maslow said that all people go through a set of stages from survival to spiritual self-actualization. We need food, then shelter, then physical health, then family, then education, then social integration, then intellectual, social and material accomplishment. Then and finally, when those are in place, we need self-actualization.). I mentioned this earlier.

◆ This includes business leaders, who are now trying to fulfil stakeholder requests, not just return shareholder dividends.

◆ New entrants to the job market have higher expectations in terms of socially responsible work, forcing employers to consider their offerings.

◆ Companies structured using hierarchies, which, in effect suppressed original thought in favour of obedience, are too slow to compete in global markets. So now we are encouraged to think, and evidence suggests that we thought about what is important and worthwhile and decided that this was more than profits for shareholders. (I called this process steering the dinosaur in *Change Activist*.)

◆ Employment for life has gone. Given the increasing impermanence of any corporate home, it is less necessary to be the robot company man. We are more inclined to take our true selves and our values to work, which over time influences the day-to-day events.

For many people, work is no longer the 'leave your true identity at the door' experience it once was. The best firms need all of you, because faster-to-market products and services won't happen through military command and control. Each cog needs to be a thinking cog. And the culture of business is becoming slowly permeated with the ordinary values of you and I, the intelligent cogs. We want to do work that feels worthwhile, and once the immediate debts have been cleared and we feel relatively secure, getting a paycheque just doesn't do that. All the time.

So, there is an osmotic process occurring. We are becoming more at work as ourselves and we are causing our companies to take notice of our concerns. As business becomes more concerned with achieving social as well as shareholder goals, as individuals we might become more able to express our spiritual core through our career. Work might be an appropriate place to look for our higher purpose. It never used to be, but maybe profit and principles could be the message that stirs our souls in the search for something bigger than ourselves. In the UK, church attendance has been in decline for the past two decades. Admittedly this is not the case in religions other than Christianity. Nor is it the case in the USA, where the majority of the population still belongs to an organized faith. But the reducing base of regular church attendees in the UK is significant. And perhaps, as that form of organized religion tunes us out, our hungry souls are tuning into something else. Some way to express the things we formerly found within religion. For example:

◆ Socially responsible investing (SRI) has doubled in size in the past three years (funds worth four billion are now placed in SRI funds).

◆ 'When people invest in a socially responsible fund they are reflecting a set of personal values and expressing a view of the world' (Mark Campanale, investment marketing manager at Henderson Global Investors, *Financial Times*, 20/21 October 2001).

It may be that the hybrid of profit and social performance could result in more people seeking to answer their calling in business. The word 'calling' has most often been used to describe a vocation – priests and nuns were 'called' and sometimes nurses and teachers or others in the caring professions. Would an ethical fund manager speak of a calling? Would a business leader who pledged to make her firm the employer of choice for all people, regardless of race or colour or sexual orientation, speak of a calling? These are not easy questions to answer, but one thing is clear. There is a shift in the financial landscape towards corporate social responsibility, improved transparency and accountability. And in my view, it doesn't matter if soultraders are the cause or the effect. The simple reality is that more of us are making career and financial investment choices based on more than short-term profit.

It is ideas which make things happen, not technology, and ideas come from people when they are being creative. Sitting at a rectangular desk under white strip lighting is not the best way to encourage such creativity. The key words for the office of the future will be creativity and flexibility. Offices will need to change to provide the creative environment employees need.

The Times, 25 January 2001

Free (or very reasonable) agent

According to a 1999 survey by Bacon and Woodrow, the number of those in manual occupations becoming self employed increased by more than 450 per cent between 1979 and 1998. Over the same period the self employed among managerial and professional workers grew by almost 300 per cent.

Richard Scase, *Britain in 2010*, Capstone, 2000

The context for your career success has changed. As ever, business leaders look for the fastest, brightest contributions. More recently, they want this contribution without paying top dollars for maintenance. What are needed are low-cost, high-contribution employees, people who are self-aware, self-motivated and clear on work/life priorities. Free agents. Or at least very reasonable. And this is the future of work.

In *Britain in 2010* (Capstone 2000), Richard Scase projects a world where freelancers take personal responsibility for employment costs, spending most of their working life on in-house performance-related projects. These contracts are negotiated, marketed and managed financially by the individual.

The individual is less likely to be part of a hierarchical management structure and more likely to be exploiting personal and social capital in a conscious way, based on pre-defined personal motivation. The market will insist that greater numbers of us wake up to the self-steered career.

What's it to be, self-steer or unclear? Your income depends on it.

A clear definition of who you are drives your ability to do who you are, to find work with purpose. This is an increasingly important part of your economic survival.

Web survey (**www.yourmomentum.com**)

What does the term 'free agent' mean for you?	Percentage (of those who answered)	1 = most common response
Working for more than one employer	12%	3
Having an internal consulting mindset in a big company	32%	2
Going freelance	56%	1
Being a junior spy	0%	

Do you define yourself as a free agent?	
Yes	64%
No	36%

Personal responsibility means you take action for the things you believe in. This is true whether you see yourself as firmly embedded in a company, or working as a freelancer or consultant or whatever kind of free agent.

"Instead of my rēsumē, I've printed out my daily horoscope for the past year. You'll see that I'm a special person who's destined for great things!"

Let's get clear on some definitions. For starters, what is a free agent? The term, coined by Daniel Pink, first appeared in 1997 in *Fast Company*. It was used to describe the freelancer, the self-employed, client-mobile worker. Free agent meant free to work with more than one company. Free of an all-embracing full-time employment contract. It grew in the optimism of the late 1990s dot.com boom, at a time when the 'e-lancer' was about to arrive and be (falsely) hailed as the next stage in career evolution. When shedloads of dot.coms became dot.bombs, many free agents became income-free agents and now companies look cool and secure again.

DO YOU CONSIDER YOURSELF TO HAVE THE POTENTIAL TO BE A FREE AGENT (DEFINED HERE AS SELF-EMPLOYED OR FREELANCE)?

Yes. I owned my own business for over 15 years. For the past two years I have been working freelance. I like the freedom and the responsibility of both being self-employed and freelance.

Michela Terrazino, creative services manager, advertising

There is a lasting legacy from that time, though; the concept of career as portfolio of activities, of greater personal work choice.
The technology tide came in and went out again, leaving behind a permanently higher watermark of changed attitudes. So, soultrader seeks to broaden the term and advance the definition to a broader constituency. Free agent in soultrader means free-of-fear agent. Able to steer based on personal freedom to choose.

Free agent: *noun*
> the free (of fear) agent mindset that causes career mobility, inside or outside full time, one organization employment

Free agency: *verb*
> the act of choosing career direction, instead of expecting a career path to be laid out by the people you work for

Free agency is a mindset. You may well be happily ensconced in the right organization for you right now. Tomorrow might be the day you need to summon up all your bravery and make the choice to do something different, new, and scary – and because that moment is almost inevitable, free agent prep is a really good idea. Choose to become a free-of-fear agent. A fear-free agent.

This is news to use now, not later. The cold wind of any passing recession blows a variety of 'they do care, really they do' scales to fall from employee eyes. That employers 'love you' (in good times) is no longer debatable. Love you as in perks, valuing diversity, paternity as well as maternity leave. However, please don't expect those warm vibes to be consistent throughout all market conditions; you are there to enhance profitability, personally mitigate the local bear market for shareholders. Just because some firms are incompetent at measuring individual bottom-line contribution doesn't mean the principle is shot. So, when those cold winds start up, get ready.

Knowing you can walk away from your desk, trusting that the next day will be a good one, is the best career-negotiating tactic known to mankind.

Compassionate detachment: Exercise

Why is it good to think of yourself as a free agent even if you are securely established in some lovely organization? The in-house free agent is incredibly valuable, what with all that big-picture view, detached improvement questing stuff and all. It is good to see that you are free to choose, even if the stack of bills at home seems to say you can't do anything alse at all.

Being able to see your career with some perspective is a soultrader essential, so this next exercise is to build your compassionate detachment muscle. Considering each story, write on a scale of one to five how close it is to your own current situation. In the empty row, summarize your current role and your summary concern right now.

The story so far... have	Close to your story? 1 = not close, 5 = very close	What concern might this person have right now?
I work as a public servant; my post is pretty secure.		Am I stuck in a rut?
I work part time as an administrator, because I want to spend time with my small children.		Am I permanently out of the career ladder?
My current situation here	5	What am I concerned about right now?
I work for a small family firm (my family) and I expect to take over from my dad in a few years' time when he retires.		Do I have the right to any other options?
I work full time for a large company doing what I wanted to do ten years ago, because I am not sure what else I could do anymore.		How do I find out what else is possible with my skills?
My work is full time, full on, and my next move is probably up the promotion ladder.		What about my life outside work, e.g. my health, seeing the family?
I work as a freelance associate to several firms, and work on a project-by-project basis.		How can I predict future earnings?
I work in the public sector and love my work, but it is exhausting and leaves no time for anything else.		Can I delegate or organize my time better to leave before 8pm?
I don't work anymore, I just do stuff that interests me when I want to, because I can afford to.		Why do I feel jealous of people who are really into what they do?
Right now I work the nightshift for a little cab firm, while also studying part time.		How can I get better grades with so little sleep?

What number makes up the majority of your responses? How do you feel about that?

The management of intellectual capital will require skills that nurture employee creativity rather than worker compliance. This will demand more open corporate communication channels and the abolition of the 'low trust' cultures that have characterised the predominant management style of 20th century British industry.

Professor Richard Scase, Britain in 2010

Free agents provide highly prized resource flexibility – they meet global business needs without causing the owners any personal development headaches. They are, of course, less loyal to the brand, the line, the board. But they are very loyal to getting the job done, which, in a hardening economy, represents a bigger agenda than keeping 100 happy staffers in Powerpoint training. They get the point and work to achieve a clear objective. They establish good relationships. They charge more because they often know more and, often, achieve more. Many companies talk about departments such as finance, HR and IT as internal consultants. One step away from outsourced free agents? People who get things done are in demand. People who know why these things need to get done are even more in demand.

DO YOU CONSIDER YOURSELF TO HAVE THE POTENTIAL TO BE A FREE AGENT (DEFINED HERE AS SELF-EMPLOYED OR FREELANCE)?

Not any more. Family commitments, lack of networking and selling skills/interest, and not sure I can see a vocation with which I could be sufficiently obsessed.

Jeremy, investment banking/securities projects

Some new rules are emerging

◆ Fewer senior sponsors will take you under their wing and explain how to win, so you have to find this out quickly on your own.

◆ You'll need to be self motivating and engaged in a purpose of your own making. There will be fewer cosy chats starting with

'What do you want to do next year, after the annual results are announced?'

◆ Individual career progression is no longer the responsibility of the employee development team in HR.

◆ It is down to the person reading this page.

◆ Therefore you need to know thyself and your unique selling proposition (USP).

◆ And how to bring this to where it can be sold most profitably.

◆ You will need the network, the skills, the knowledge and the self-confidence to get your unique message across.

◆ Then have the wit and wisdom to do it socially sustainably.

Easy, right? Clearly not. The university degree and the first five years you spent as a trainee assistant senior person didn't give you any warning that the world was going to change. I didn't see any newsflash about the business community change of heart. Companies that a few years ago wanted lifelong loyalty seem to automatically want to outsource, just because a desk and a career plan are now overheads.

You, the staffer, are the expensive option compared with free agents who have their own desks and career plans. You may well be more loyal, but that isn't always the deciding factor. The deciding factor is most experience and skill, most enthusiasm, at least cost. Because that, for the owners and senior team and shareholders, means job done, profit made, money reinvested, move on.

So it seems especially useful to know what motivates and creates your unique self, now that this colder wind blows through our future earning plans. The results are clear to see. Career paths have become less structured, with fewer head-office HR overseers. Organizations have become loose networks, where staffers work alongside and sometimes inside alliances, third-party suppliers, and preferred partners, with freelancers and consultants. The freelancers now seem to be covered by the term free agents and the world is full of them.

Us. Consider how far you have already come in this job; surely independence is one of your options right now? But it does need to be authentic independence. More than profit.

Hollywood is a place where they'll pay you a thousand dollars for a kiss and fifty cents for your soul.

Marilyn Monroe

We have a much better chance of thriving through the transition if the job is also our life purpose. As I said in the introduction, even if you are currently plumbed into some corporate life-support system, it is an excellent idea to know how to breathe your own air as a free agent. Internal free agents who can bring some kind of consulting perspective to the job are the ones who survive post-merger, post-downsizing. Unlike those who trust in some greater, compassionate strategy and quietly await the e-mail with career instructions and a new organizational model.

So you maybe need to catch up. My aim is to help you work some personal things out, so you know what you have to trade as a free agent. The more you know yourself, the more certainty and purpose in your public life, at your desk, on the hospital ward, in front of your own clients, in the charity fundraising department, in your home. Wherever. The free agent is a role you can choose to play. Either as self-employed, consulting knowledge worker, or as the organization-based hero who needs to get a bit more clarity and control over your path. It is possible to access more of your inner resources. Learning how to access those inner resources just isn't a well-honed skill. We perhaps have too many not nice but necessary well-honed skills – like feigning fun when the new boss turns unexpectedly humorous, or accessing personal e-mails during the latest office crisis when you're meant to be finding the hole in the spreadsheets. What about finding the reason for the hole in your happiness this year? What about how you are?

One consistent theme as we do this soultrade exploration is the need to create career options that produce socially responsible profit at personal level. Socially responsible profit at a personal level. That's right. Let's take this from another perspective.

The good company idea is gaining ground. Within that, the good team is raising its responsible head above the 'head down, just do the job' parapet. The good team being, for example, one that chooses to paint the local nursery during the three-day offsite instead of spending the final day chez boss paid booze.

The good team is one that abseils, en masse, past the finance manager's window before asking him for a cheque for the local children's charity.

But the good free agent? Not so much evidence. Perhaps because that isn't a well-honed skill for most of us either. Surely it is worthwhile though? If firms are finding it is well worth their while to play the ethical card, surely it is well worth your time adding that aspect to your portfolio of free-agent offerings? Makes sense. Defined at the most simple level as 'the consultant you can trust' and at the most complex level as 'the person who helps business leaders make more money by solving world poverty', you can't really argue with socially responsible profit at a personal level.

Evidence suggests that a particularly prized breed of free agent is the self-directing, social free agent. Of whom there will be more later. Whatever you hope to achieve, your personal strategy will structure the doing of it.

Free agents are emotionally independent of their jobs and their current financial boss. How? Because they realize that although work assignments change, the key elements of their personal strategy remain the same.

Free agents are in constant transition, moving on to the next, bigger, better thing while delivering benefits here and now. In plain talk, getting things done in order of priority. Free agents are not scared to let go of old skills, old contacts, and old comfort blankets. Watching free agents, and I have worked alongside a lot of them, I realize that this transition process is their career. Finding the right assignment, the right client, trying to negotiate the right fees. Working out how to stand out. Using one task as a lever to get to a juicy assignment where you get to do the thing you love most, with your favourite people, for the most money.

For free agents, career transition is core business.

Finding the right market niche, and scratching it.

How can you find your own individual career niche? How long will that fit last? How useful is your soul in determining those answers?

Whatever your role, or profession or quest, I recommend you learn to think like a free agent. Why? Because your self-steered career is more likely to succeed than the career steered by a committee of bosses, because you care more about what happens to you. The career path of a fear-free agent is typically less secure, more rewarded. The career path of a staffer for life is less secure, less rewarded. You choose. You can reasonably expect other benefits when you trade-in your job security.

There are too many chances to win in this life to ever rule yourself out. So how can you get free-agent mindset? Phone this freephone number to buy the complete set? Er, no.

Free-agent mindset starts with one thing: I am responsible for what happens in my life. Not the boss, my wife, the bank, the kids, the merger, the mortgage, the markets, the weather or Murphy's law. I am responsible, I am in control of my life and I choose to be on the right path. Wow.

Being a fulfilled free agent in the outer world is a direct result of being a free agent first of all in your head.

We self-justify uncool or unsatisfying jobs at personal cost. Self-deception about the lack of fulfilment is remarkably common.

Career owner, or renter?

The old ownership club doesn't have a monopoly on our knowledge. The grip is potentially being loosened by the combined effects of technology, the sheer weight of numbers of diverse people entering the global market. Oh, and the promise of a generation with less respect, less concern for personal status compared with learning.

This means that our mindset is more of a clue to our eventual earnings. Do we choose to take our careers to heart (and soul) and create what we really want? Or do we choose to keep work at a distance from our hearts and souls and remain essential renters of our career destiny?

My life might be an example of how to have a good time starting from outside the owners' club. Second-generation Irish, queer, female and reasonably wealthy from a ten-year adventure in corporate life. Which was impossible 100 years ago. My daily adventure then would have been: 'Could you hang on to the twelfth child [said as a request to the first child] darling, while I'm out digging crop to give away to the landlord?'

Being born outside the owners' club 100 years ago meant living and dying outside the owners' club. You can forget your cosy self-actualization scenario there. Anyway. Here we all are, here and now. Less enslaved, able to choose the degree of mental proximity to 100 years ago, and more able to steer our careers.

Now that we are moving away from historical choice shortages, we have to adjust to this world of expanded personal career choice. Choice that is emerging alongside that loosening grip on capital. There has been a historical leap from the jobs of owners and the jobs of non-owners to a whole range of jobs where the boundaries are blurred. Supermarket assistants potentially earn more than the landed gentry they occasionally serve due to the allocation of shares and some prudent buying by the employees. Small-technology-business owners often take home less than the freelance skill specialists they employ to cut code. What you do is less a function of the family you were born into 100 years ago than the range of specialist skills you choose to amass. This also means the slow attrition of less lucrative or cool careers.

Upstairs, downstairs anyone? A career as a servant? Well-tried path, lots of role models. You can slip right into the template, almost no pre-planning required. No thanks. We are learning how to make our own independence. We choose not to buy the pre-made lives that our parents and grandparents were told were all on offer.

The shift means this. You get more chance to achieve your destiny through more choice of work.

The bad news is that choice brings responsibility – to yourself. The good news is that you are able to make great choices – you just haven't accessed all the ways to do it just yet.

Cynics talk about wage slavery – I am a bit more optimistic. I think some of us were born indentured, not enslaved. And we are allowed more dissent than our parents in the course of this working life. Witness the anti-globalization protests in Seattle and Genoa, the rise of the anxious consumer.

By bringing personal authenticity to work with us, is it possible that you and I can make changes to the way big business operates? What do you think?

It might be that we are dissatisfied with the lack of cheques and balances for global trade. Our TV screens have filled up with images of uncaring business, inhuman working conditions, we read about the widening wealth gap between big-business owners and the global workforce – so surely some dissatisfaction is normal. But is the fundamental business deal up for negotiation?

My suspicion is that the sentiments expressed at Seattle and Genoa and other anti-globalization protests are going to take a long time to convert into a majority business agenda. My fear is that the dissent might be theme-park dissent, where you have the flavours and sensations of change without removing root causes of injustice. I really hope not, but it seems that the lucky owners of all there is to exploit and sell on Planet Earth are a relatively stable community. Our dissent doesn't seem to alter the fundamental rules of ownership. If you look at the last 200 years, an amazingly constant group of good ol' boys sits pretty with the family name on the land deeds (meaning ownership of the natural commodities, e.g. the oil that makes the big bucks).

So the change, the big destiny for our generation, is perhaps most likely to come through personal awakening: the private understanding that each of us can create a new way of working that doesn't harm, and that we will be more personally fulfilled if we find a way to contribute to our nearest communities as well as working to make a personal profit.

Soultrading is a personally responsible approach to making profit – it welcomes personal profit because it can create more options for fulfilment. The gamble I am taking is to say that when people realize there is a way to make personal profit without reducing the quality of life for anyone else, then something changes. The message our parents had – get what you can and don't worry about anyone else – was based on a different global economy. Paradoxically, there is less security now and more free agents willing to fly solo through the business world. The road from mental indenture to free agent requires a soultrader outlook to succeed. Profit for profit's sake is a short-term agenda.

Two career groups: which one works?

The rise of free agents is causing a two-way split, and two categories of experience are emerging in the new economy. Work is either perceived as:

◆ A means of self-actualization

Or

◆ A means of financial survival.

Rarely equally both. Let me explain.

You either look to your job to express who you are, your identity developing through career challenge, or your job is the way you earn money to be able to afford to express yourself in other ways.

Gut feel, which are you? My contention is that the best jobs go to those who see work as a vehicle for self-actualization because they are the jobs that have been expanded to include more social and spiritual objectives. More education for more people equals more expectation perhaps?

The logical step on is this: your attitude toward work will determine access to the best jobs. Jobs linked to the highest purpose of humanity are more likely to be high earning. Remember the headhunter who said greatness meant wider emotional, as well as technical intelligence?

The professional classes, typically educated and from a more comfortable background, have always had job satisfaction on the list of things to do this life. The manual labourers, or unskilled resources did not. The unskilled job was simply whatever had to be done to earn money and, although each job has its social aspect, it was less likely that unskilled work gave intrinsic motivation. Now it is also true that the lines are beginning to blur. Information technology, for example, requires lots of physical maintenance, lots of jobs that are neither professional nor unskilled. The helpdesk technician, the call-centre assistant, the hardware installation team – where do they fit into the hierarchy? Skilled, yes, but not professionals. OK.

This is a change to the old order when a financially independent elite enjoyed greater freedom to choose a career linked to self-actualization. Traditionally, music and the arts have been the domain of those of us who are able to earn less and take time to train for a less lucrative career – certainly in the UK. Is it possible that the classless society is expressed in more demand for self-actualization at work?

What does this mean to you? It means that you need to define your expectations of life, and work, more clearly.

Because it would be a real shame to wake up in five years and realize that all that time could have been well spent getting to really understand who you are, but you just didn't realize. How do you wake up? First of all realize that the world of work has changed. Yes, even where you work. And you have the chance to choose, more than ever before.

The two-way split of self-actualizers or earn-to-survive workers could be taken into smaller pieces. Perhaps this 'true path is the new black' environment has four distinct categories of people:

Self-actualizing

1   Those of us who do not need to earn a living. We seem to inevitably set about becoming celebrities. Celebrity becomes the career of choice for the people who do not need a career (the party-throwing owners).

2   Those of us who are consciously achieving our destiny, are clear on our life's work, and are energized with purpose (the soultraders).

Survival

1   Those of us who are doing this job, right now because it seems the only available career option (the economic survivors).

2 Those of us who are not quite sure if the job is right, or of our destiny, and are a bit nervous of the whole subject, because what if the answer means change (the frightened brights)?

Now it is possible to be a combination, or all, or none. There is no hierarchy. We perhaps get to touch down in each category through the course of a long career.

chapter six
12-day life purpose plan

Do you want to be a soultrader? Do you want a career energized with purpose? You can make it happen, and you can start right here and now.

This chapter brings together the key soultrader exercises into a 12-day plan – which you can work on successive days or over a period of time. It is really helpful to work through these with someone to discuss the various responses and offer insight.

You may have started to think these through, or make notes as they appeared on the earlier pages.

Day 1 Finding fire and focus

Fire

First of all write down about ten ideas off the top of your head on how you could set the world on fire. They don't all have to be about your career. Maybe use these questions to help:

◆ The audience thunder their applause. From centrestage you look out at a sea of appreciative faces. You feel elated, delighted. What just happened?

- Close your eyes and see yourself being awarded the Nobel Prize. You are modest and succinct in victory. Why did you receive it?

- Your best friend phones up and says, 'Wow – I just read about you in the paper.' What did she/he just read about?

- You look at the letter containing your examination results and see the most amazing words. What are they?

- Over a new year's drink, you look back on the best year of your life. What was the best bit?

- You arrive in heaven and find your name with an entry next to it, summarizing the contribution you made to humanity while you were alive. What does it say?

Rank your answers from one the brightest fire, to ten the least bright.

1

2

3

4

5

6

7

8

9

10

Focus: this is important to me.

Consider what you normally do, and pick your top five.

Now try to put them in order of priority.

My top five focus:

Next we bring the two exercises together.

My combined fire and focus list

Top five fire	Top five focus
1	1
2	2
3	3
4	4
5	5

OK. Now I want you to map these on to a model that brings together the fire and focus priorities.

Fire and focus model
To identify your life priorities

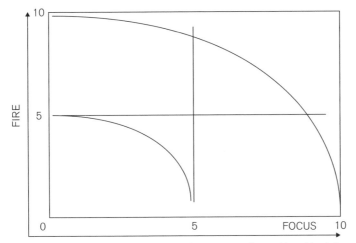

What am I
passionate
about?

se the vertical
axis to rank
ur life's desire.

FIRE

FOCUS

What are the things you really want/need to do?

First start with the answers you marked 4 or 5. Write your fire
choices on the left side, your focus choices on the right. They should
lie within the bottom left arch. Then your answers marked 2 and 3.
Again, write your fire choices on the left side, your focus choices on
the right. They should lie within the middle band. Finally, the
answers you marked as 1. Fire on the left, focus on the right. These
answers should appear in the top right-hand corner. You should now
see a prioritized model.

high fire + high focus = your purpose

Day 2 Feeling rich

Do you feel trapped by lack of money?

As soultraders, you and I are responsible for our financial wellbeing and happiness.

Financial purpose

What do the roots of my experience say about me and money?

E.g. access to finance, my habits, my attitude:

- In the past

- Right now

- In the future?

What does the root of my passion say about me and money?

- What must I have?

- What excites or repulses me about financial success?

- What are my passionate extravagances?

What does the root of my trust say about me and money?

- Do I trust the future to include financial success?

- Do I believe I am destined to be poor?

- Do I have a self-imposed earnings limit?

- What are my family views?

What does the root of my learning say about me and money?

- How do I rate in terms of financial awareness – honestly?

- Could I become clued up about saving and investment

- Could I learn to take financial control of my life?

Day 3 Reduce the skim rate

When the Buddha was asked what was different after he found enlightenment, he replied, 'I am awake.' The next exercise helps you soultrade not soulskim through life.

Exercise

Might it help to forward-plan your next month to kick the skim habit?

Today's date:

Significant events coming up this week:

Next week:

Next month:

Against each one, you can choose to:

◆ Check it out in advance – what is actually planned versus what is more likely to happen.

◆ Figure out the desired outcome.

◆ Be awake and alert during the event.

◆ Record some of the things you get from it.

◆ And follow through.

What language do you naturally think in – soultrade or soulskim? Take one event in one week and find out what a big difference this choice will make.

Day 4 Stop the self-sabotage using innerware

Good and easy or mean and hard?

Are you open to working life being good and easy, or open to it being mean and hard? During one day, catch the phrases you use about yourself. It might be 'I'm so crap at numbers'. It might be 'typical, it doesn't work' or 'I don't deserve that.' Write down at least five.

Next to them write down the opposites. Use words that work for you. First of all, identify your top self-sabotage phrases. Then their opposites. Then say the opposite to yourself as much as you can.

Yes, it can feel weird. Our brains work like computers, literally on instructions, so we need better innerware to operate them.

Phrases I use most often	The opposite
e.g. 'I'm always useless at …'	e.g. 'I'm always good at …'

Day 5 What does it all mean?

Today bring together all the material you have collated so far, and just have a think about what it all means.

Where do you think your life's purpose springs from?

Where	Answer: yes, no or maybe
Football	
My soul	
The financial goals of the place I work for	
Mum and dad	
Don't care	
God, Jesus, Mohammed, Buddha or another religious source	
University	
My friends	
Don't know	
Haven't got one	
The kids	
Somewhere in my mind	
Other	

Day 6 Uncovering my passions

Look at the example from Steve's life. Now consider your own life, with these questions:

Roots of purpose: passion	Questions	My answers
	What part of your work do you feel most passionate about?	
Passion sub-root: action (defined as the ability to do something, rather than talk about it)	What has caused you to take the most important actions in your career?	
	Why?	
Passion sub-root: choice (defined as the ability to select the most heartfelt option)	Describe the choices you feel exist in your career right now. Is that more or less than you want to have?	
Passion sub-root: change (defined as the capacity to get excited about new situations and creating career flexibility to take on new challenges)	Do you feel able to make changes in your life to stay passionate about what you do?	
	How does this manifest itself?	

Day 7 Career highs and lows so far

On a piece of paper, draw a line. Start on the left, which can be any point in your working life, for example when you left school or university, or your first job. The line finishes at where you are today. Starting from the left, write down the big events in your career: a new job, a promotion. Also write down the big lows. Write the year next to each one. The line represents a neutral time in your life. If it helps, write zero on the line and write each high or low to scale. Now join the dots.

Career highs and lows

Me aged _____ Me now

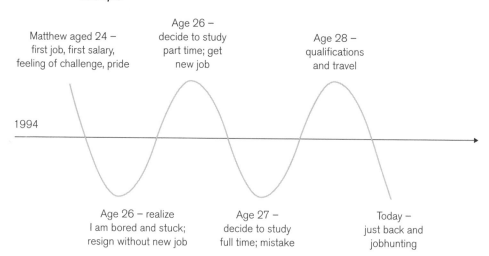

Example

Matthew aged 24 – first job, first salary, feeling of challenge, pride

Age 26 – decide to study part time; get new job

Age 28 – qualifications and travel

1994

Age 26 – realize I am bored and stuck; resign without new job

Age 27 – decide to study full time; mistake

Today – just back and jobhunting

Day 8 Learning to trust life

Refresh yourself about Emma's example (see p. 92).

(see p. 92)

What does the root of trust tell me?

My root: trust	Questions	My answers
	Can you tell me what is working well in your life right now?	
Trust sub-root: **expectation**	What are you expecting the next six months to hold?	
Trust sub-root: **patience**	What other options do you have – is there something you want to do more that might need some planning and care?	
	Might that be possible?	
Trust sub-root: **confidence**	What are you hoping to do if you get on well with those ambitions?	

Day 9 Writing my own career script

You are the author of the scary story. So you can be the author of the success story.

A first consideration, then, when trying for the work, job or life that you most want is to consider your own ability to write the script.

Against your fire-and-focus priorities, whatever they are write down:

1   The scary story

What am I most scared about – what is stopping me from taking action?

What are my fears? What is the worst that can happen? What might go wrong?

I am scared that if I try for this, the following might happen:

I am worried about.

2   The success story

What are my hopes and dreams? What is the best thing that can happen? What might be fabulous?

It is possible that if I try this, the following brilliant things might happen:

I am excited about:

Day 10 What does my destiny look like?

Is this job my true destiny?

Please circle one answer:

1 I have a clear idea of where my career is heading.
Agree/Disagree/Not sure

2 I know what I have to do to get to my career goals.
Agree/Disagree/Not sure

3 My day-to-day work is aimed at achieving those career goals.
Agree/Disagree/Not sure

4 My career purpose allows time for more than work. (e.g. family, sport, travel).
Agree/Disagree/Not sure

5 I'm known for the fact I'm living true to my authentic self.
Agree/Disagree/Not sure

6 My career goals are financially sound.
Agree/Disagree/Not sure

7 My job feeds my soul as well as my body.
Agree/Disagree/Not sure

If you agree with more than four of those, great. You have decided where you want to go – and you are travelling closer with each day. Less than four? Take a look at the fire-and-focus exercise and start telling your friends to expect some changes …

Day 11 Create an authentic CV

Soultrader CV template

Answer these questions with examples and humour:

What are your most important qualifications?	
What is your most important qualification in terms of personal authenticity?	
How, when and where are you happiest?	
What are your career highlights? Are they natural or tinted?	
What makes you stand out from others (think about service, contribution and care here)?	
What personal characteristics cause you to be a reputable candidate (e.g. your great project skills, sense of humour)?	
What do you believe to be your greatest accomplishment?	
Who was impacted by that – what did it mean to them?	
What is the most inspiring thing that you have ever done?	
Can you quantify those accomplishments in terms of life enhancement as well as figures?	
What, in your view, does the world need now (in addition to love, sweet love)?	
What do you contribute to making the world a better place (i.e. if you were going to save the world, which part would you choose to save first)?	

▶

Why, overall, do you believe your reputation to be overwhelmingly positive?	
Describe the skills of people who would create a perfect team for you to work with.	
Finally, who loves you? Tell us about your network.	

Answering those will set you up to perform in any soundbite situation. Now continue day 11's good work with a role play interview.

Interview for the best job ever

◆ As a manager, what do you strongly believe in?

◆ What gives you greatest satisfaction at work?

◆ Tell me about your success.

What are your answers to these questions?

Day 12 Allowing success to happen

You might be starting to have some new perspective on your career and your life. Today, the final day of the purpose plan, gather together all the exercises plus any additional material you have on the subject of your life's purpose.

Collate everything and spend an hour reviewing, asking yourself these questions, and affirming these statements.

◆ Have I decided to stay or go?

◆ How can I draw on my roots to make that decision
   (my experience, passion, learning and trust)?

◆ What is the best part of my current work?

◆ How can I create work that feels even more fulfilling?

◆ Who do I most enjoy working with?

◆ Why?

- My best career decisions so far have been:

- I really do expect happiness, fulfilment and success.

- It's time for me to be happier.

- What will I do first? My ideas are:

I wish you a brilliant future.

Finding a career full of happiness, fulfilment and success is a great adventure and each one of us can do it.

resources

For a soultrader reading list, check out www.yourmomentum.com

For information on soultrader seminars and events contact
carmelmcconnel@btinternet.com

soultrader soundtrack

Music for your soultrader.

Side 1

If you're ready (come go with me)   *Staples Singers (1973)*
Take me to the river   *Al Green (?)*
The real life   *Raven Maize (2001)*
These sounds fall into my mind   *The Bomb (1997)*
I was made to love her   *Stevie Wonder (1966)*
You're free   *Ultra Nate (1998)*
Forget me nots   *Patrice Rushen (1982)*
Hard work   *John Handy (1976)*
Harvest for the world   *Isley Brothers (1976)*
Young fresh 'n' new   *Kelis (Timo mass remix) (2001)*
Running away   *Roy Ayers (1977)*

Side 2

Big love   *Pete Heller (1999)*
Rapture   *Blondie (1980)*
Flawless   *The Ones (2001)*
Feeling groovy   *Simon and Garfunkel (1970)*
Ready to go   *Republica (1996)*
Go   *Moby (1992)*
Uptight (everything's alright)   *Stevie Wonder (1965)*
Don't give up   *Bryan Adams featuring Chicane (2000)*
Best of my love   *The Emotions (1977)*

Sun is shining   *Bob Marley (remix 2000)*
Voyager   *Daft Punk (2001)*

These are the songs that have helped me – maybe they can inspire, energize, animate, get inside your groove to the point where you want to move.

Anyway, I hope you like them.

momentum prescription – Let Us Help You Work Out Which Book Will Suit Your Symptoms

Feel stuck in a rut? Something wrong and need help doing something about it?

◆ If you need tools to help making changes in your life: **coach yourself** (a good general guide to change)

◆ If you are considering dramatic career change: **snap, crackle or stop**

◆ If you need to work out what you'd like to be doing and how to get there: **be your own career consultant**

◆ If you need help making things happen and tackling the 'system' at work/in life: **change activist**

Feel that you can never make decisions and you just let things 'happen'?

◆ If you need help making choices: **the big difference**

◆ If you want to feel empowered and start making things happen for yourself: **change activist**

Feel life is too complicated and overwhelming?

◆ If you need help working through office politics and complexity: **clued up**

◆ If you need a kick up the backside to get out of your commerce-induced coma: **change activist**

◆ If you need an amusing and very helpful modern life survival guide: **innervation**

◆ If you never have enough time or energy to get things done or think properly: **mental space**

Feel like you might be in the wrong job?

◆ If you want help finding your destiny job and inspiration to make that dramatic career change: **snap, crackle or stop**

◆ If you feel like you aren't doing a job that is really 'what you are about': **soultrader**

◆ If you are struggling with the 'do something worthwhile OR make money dilemma': **change activist**

Feel that you're not the person/leader you should be?

◆ If you want to be the kind of person others want to follow: **lead yourself**

◆ If you need help becoming the person you've always wanted to be: **reinvent yourself**

◆ If you want to work out everything you've got to offer, and how to improve that: **grow your personal capital**

Feel you need help getting your ideas into action?

◆ If the problem is mainly other people, lack of time and the messiness of life: **clued up**

◆ If the problem is communicating your thinking: **hey you!**

◆ If the problem is more ideas than time and you are a bit overwhelmed with work: **mental space**

◆ If the problem is making change in your life: **coach yourself**

Feel you aren't projecting yourself and managing your career as well as you should?

◆ If you'd like to be the kind of person people think of first: **managing brand me**

◆ If you'd like people to listen to your ideas more readily: **hey you!**

◆ If you'd like to come across as the person you really are inside: **soultrader**

◆ If you need general help in changing the way you work/life: **coach yourself**

◆ If you need help working out what you've got and how best to use it: **float you**

Feel you'd like to be much more creative and a real 'ideas person'

◆ If you need inspiration on how to be innovative and think creatively: **innervation**

◆ If you need help spreading your ideas and engendering support: **hey you!**